EXORCISM

The Removal of Evil Influences

Also by Martin Israel:

Life Eternal (SPCK 1993)
Angels: Messengers of Grace (SPCK 1995)

EXORCISM
The Removal of Evil Influences

MARTIN ISRAEL

First published in Great Britain 1997
Society for Promoting Christian Knowledge
Holy Trinity Church
Marylebone Road
London NW1 4DU

British Library Cataloguing-in-Publication Data

A catalogue record of this book is available from
the British Library

ISBN 0-281-04974-2

Typeset by Pioneer Associates, Perthshire
Printed in Great Britain by
Redwood Books, Trowbridge, Wiltshire

Contents

—~~∿∿AAAAΩAAAA∿∿—

Publisher's Note

—————

If readers of this book feel in need of the ministry of deliverance, they may seek advice from the Churches' Fellowship for Psychical and Spiritual Studies at:

The Rural Workshop
South Road
North Somercotes
LOUTH
Lincolnshire
LN11 7PT.

Readers could also contact their Anglican diocesan office and ask to be put in touch with the diocesan convenor of the deliverance team.

Preface

————〜〜ᴨᴨᴧ◉ᴧᴨᴨ〜〜————

The psychic field is the source of perennial delight to those looking for a new stimulus in their lives; to those who are quite content with matters as they stand at present any anomalous phenomenon causes fear amounting to great agitation. Psychic phenomena are typically anomalous, their abnormality and irregularity tending to disturb the peace and quiet of the vicinity. The question always remains: are they real in their own right or merely manifestations of environmental disturbances or mental ill health among those whom they afflict?

I have attempted to address this question with respect to well-known phenomena such as poltergeist activity, spontaneous impressions of communication from the other side of death, and irregularities in the behaviour of a certain type of person generally termed 'psychic'. The field is enormous, and rather than stretching it out interminably with various specious anecdotes, I have remained doggedly close to what is actually known about the subject, using, as always, the Bible as my textbook about phenomena that bear the stamp of truth. The more psychically aware one becomes in one's own life, the less difficult does it become to believe the scriptural evidence in its own right without needing to accept a fundamentalist bias.

This book is addressed to those whose attention has

been arrested by anomalous phenomena, especially those that seem to inhabit the murky world of relationships between the clearly living and the more opaque realm between the living and those who may be described as 'discarnate'. These phenomena cannot be accurately defined in terms of our five senses nearly so well as by the emotional upheaval they stir up within us. A person of psychic sensitivity has the gift of awareness of emanations arising from other people in the general environment.

1

Exorcism and Deliverance

Exorcism entails the ejection of an undesirable psychic entity from a person or a locality, whereas deliverance is concerned more with the handing over of the entity to God's care. In practice the two actions merge, but in principle there is a world of difference between 'casting out a demonic spirit' into the outer realms where there is 'wailing and grinding of teeth', to quote a favourite analogy in Matthew's Gospel, and bringing such a spirit into the loving influence of God's compassion and caring. The first way leaves the vicious entity in a state of fury (and fear) where it can still remain a considerable menace to unprotected humans (and other forms of life also), whereas the second way leaves all final judgements to the Creator alone. In the end I cannot believe that God has created any total failures, even if in the short term our world is a morass of suffering and cruelty. The question is: how are we to respond to the various forms of existence that we meet? Some are living forms that we can immediately recognize, but others are intangible except to inner senses that most of us have never been taught to accept, except in terms of distrust.

At this point certain definitions are worth citing:

Occult   –   hidden from physical and intellectual sight.

1

Psychic	–	shown by its emotional and disruptive content despite its occult character.
Demonic	–	of occult character but decidedly evil intent.
Spiritual beings	–	hidden from our personal view but shown by their effect on our way of life with special reference to the soul as acted on by God.
Charismatic	–	a word frequently misused, but properly meaning an absolute openness to the Holy Spirit without our getting in the way.
Clairvoyance	–	faculty of seeing mentally what is happening or exists out of sight.
Magic	–	the employment of psychic powers for purely selfish motives.

A demonic spirit is always evil, but the degree of harm it produces is connected to whether it is merely misplaced, or whether it has rejected its faith for personal reasons.

A discarnate human spirit is disposed in a self-centred way after that person's death. A demonic spirit is evil when its intentions are destructive, leading to hatred and vicious intentions in the victims. If merely misplaced, it shows signs of bewilderment that may produce a leap of discernment in is victim. It rarely produces an atmosphere of evil, but there may be severe confusion.

It is on this level that we may begin to grasp the deeper meaning of reality. So St Paul writes in 2 Corinthians 4.16–5.4:

No wonder we do not lose heart! Though our outward humanity is in decay, yet day by day we are inwardly

2

renewed. Our troubles are slight and short-lived, and their outcome is an eternal glory which far outweighs them, provided our eyes are fixed, not on the things that are seen, but on the things that are unseen; for what is seen is transient, what is unseen is eternal. We know that if the earthly frame that houses us today is demolished, we possess a building which God has provided – a house not made by human hands, eternal and in heaven. In the present body we groan, yearning to be covered by our heavenly habitation put on over this one, in the hope that, being thus clothed, we shall not find ourselves naked. We groan indeed, we who are enclosed within this earthly frame; we are oppressed because we do not want to have the old body stripped off. What we want is to be covered by the new body put on over it, so that our mortality may be absorbed into life immortal.

It seems that the deeper experience of evil, so strong as to threaten our very existence, is closely related to the emanation that proceeds from another person or their habitation. Superficially these people may seem very pleasant, yet there is something about them that occasions a feeling of unease within us. We are intuitively aware that all is not right within them, and we cringe from their proffered friendship to retire into our own solitude (and safety), where we may encounter the Divine Presence in a state of complete confidence. The person themself is not necessarily evil, but is rather the plaything of demonic sources that spread unhappiness through them among all those people whom they may know, at least for a variable period of time. In a community of people such 'infested' individuals can be easily discerned by those who are psychically sensitive, but we are all well advised to beware of criticizing others until we ourselves are clear of problems. We are warned in the course of the Sermon on the Mount to desist from judging others until we ourselves are less personally impure.

3

Do not judge, and you will not be judged. For as you judge others, so you will yourselves be judged, and whatever measure you deal out to others will be dealt to you. Why do you look at the speck of sawdust in your brother's eye, with never a thought for the plank in your own? How can you say to your brother, 'Let me take the speck out of your eye,' when all the time there is a plank in your own? You hypocrite! First take the plank out of your own eye, and then you will see clearly to take the speck out of your brother's. (Matthew 7.1–5)

Psychic attentiveness is a special grace, a gift from God to apparently exceptional people, but I believe that it is present to a greater or lesser extent in the awareness of all people provided their eyes are fixed on 'unseen things', to quote 2 Corinthians 4.18 once more. This grace is maligned especially by those individuals who are ignorant, prejudiced and intolerant, to say nothing of those who, apparently unaware of it in themselves, seek to disprove its existence or beneficence in those who seem to be uncannily gifted in predicting future events that later indeed prove to be true. We are most likely to have use of this 'occult' grace when we sit in self-giving quietness before God, whether in devout, silent prayer or in active, attentive concern for a fellow creature who is troubled and desperately needs our help.

The gift is indeed a grace from God, but we have to play our own part if it is to show itself to its greatest value. This means divesting ourselves of all desires of self-gratification, so that we can neither claim a special benefit from the work nor bask in reflected glory: 'No one can serve two masters; for either he will hate the first and love the second, or he will be devoted to the first and despise the second. You cannot serve God and money [or mammon, the god of money]' (Matthew 6.24). A felicitous working arrangement between the things of this world and eternity itself is the object of the world's desire. Mammon is a very powerful psychic entity that flows out to us in the form of a personal desire for possessions and money. These, though not to be discarded in the world of matter in which we lead our earthly lives, are of use only in transient things that feed the body. When they impinge on the soul, which is the seat of our value judgements, they have a subtle corrupting influence, and soon they wear down the beauty of the personality. Thus Jesus warns us, 'Do not fear those who kill the body, but cannot kill the soul. Fear him rather who is able to destroy both body and soul in hell' (Matthew 10.28).

Here we approach the evil influence of the psychic dimension: it corrupts by enticing us to yield to the lesser – the world of matter and pleasure – instead of aspiring to the greater – the knowledge of God which passes all human understanding. It does this by leading us away from the life of material limitation, whose end is necessarily transient and encompassed in bodily death with little apparent hope of any survival of the personality beyond a form that seems completely enclosed in the desires of the flesh, blood and bone. But there is also a more attractive psychic world that carries us forward from the purely physical aspects of our personality, so that we may catch a glimpse of something of a life ahead of us. This view of reality is derided by the materialist as pure delusion, while denounced by the 'religious' type of person as dangerous trafficking in dubious spirits whose testimony is not to be trusted.

The knowledge of God is indeed derived from the psychic realm, but it claims no material value for itself. On the contrary, it leads us from all personal objectives in order to play our part in the glorification of the world under the aegis of God. Therefore the psychic realm can be one of selfish delusion or altruistic endeavour on behalf of all creatures in their upward trail to the presence of God within themselves. This is what Colossians 1.27 describes as 'Christ in you, the hope of glory'. This is the blue light of transparent character that shows itself when we are close to the Divine Presence in deep, prayerful meditation. This is nothing that we can conjure up by our own imagination and will. On the contrary, when we are still and in self-giving attention to the Divine Presence we are most able to move beyond our customary self-centred consciousness, and then our inner awareness is cleansed of trivial desire.

Self-centred desire is the real basis of psychic illusion, in which our own desires, lusts and avarice take on the misleading character of divine inspiration. This, of course, is the way in which the demonic agents assume the character of forces of light. But their light does not possess the consistent, penetrating quality of spiritual light, which is the psychic way in which we can identify the divine origin of the light. I am always reminded of a favourite biblical quotation, 'God is love; he who dwells in love is dwelling in God, and God in him' (1 John 4.16). If the psychic light of spiritual emanation is clear and blue, the psychic light of garish, personal desire is above all else a glaring, whitish colour, but it lacks the delicacy of spiritual illumination. It scintillates but it does not enlighten.

We are most open to the divine grace – and therefore aware of the wiles of the demonic entities that inhabit the lower reaches of the psychic realm – when our minds are free from personal vice and most open to a charitable influx from the world around us. The seven deadly sins – which at least to some extent are opposites of that harvest of the Holy Spirit enumerated in Galatians 5.22–3 – are pride, covetousness, lust, anger, gluttony, envy and sloth. These have to be confronted with honesty and courage. If we try to slip out of our moral responsibility by evading our psychic darkness and looking to others for our guidance and help, we find that we sink into a state of moral impotence in which we fall victim to the forces of destruction in the world, and become increasingly incapable of making any decisions of our own.

When we accept the existence of points of darkness within ourself, we can respond positively to God's grace by opening ourselves to it and letting it play upon our areas of spiritual and psychic weakness. Once we become open to the strife within ourself, we can begin to pray earnestly and effectually in a state of liberation and detached loving concern for all the world's creatures which we all know in our own native incarnational experience. This includes both personal relations and the wider world around us. Our time on earth provides invaluable insight into how we move in the intricate maze of our relationships with other people, and through them with other forms of life (especially animal) that in the usual course of events we would scarcely notice at all. This sheds light on our natural tendency to remain oblivious of the needs of our fellow creatures until we are forced to share in the experience common to all humans. The parable of the prodigal son (Luke 10.29–37) emphasizes this on the level of personal experience. Only thus do we know what it feels like to be out in the cold.

The manifest failure of a Christian healing ministry at least on a personal level, is described in 2 Corinthians 12.1–10. About fourteen years after St Paul had had a very momentous experience of divine revelation, he was given a 'thorn in the flesh', which he identified with a messenger from Satan sent to buffet him, to prevent him from becoming unduly elated. On three occasions he prayed fervently to be rid of this problem, but the answer he received was: 'My grace is all you need; power is most fully seen in weakness.' Paul was therefore happy to boast of his weaknesses, because then the power of Christ would rest on him. So he was content with a life of weakness, insult, hardship, persecution and distress, all for Christ's sake. He made the final dogmatic declaration: 'for when I am weak, then I am strong.' The nature of Paul's 'thorn in the flesh' remains unknown; it was most likely a medical condition of spasmodic attacks that embarrassed the great apostle to the Gentiles. But one thing is certain to me: all our fullness of being depends on the presence and love of Christ in our lives. 'On him the whole body depends. Bonded and held together by every constituent joint, the whole frame grows through the proper functioning of each part, and builds itself up in love' (Ephesians 4.16). It is this constant, compact and indissoluble union of all creation – whether in the body, the mind or the soul – that is effected by psychic interdependence. And yet, having made this categorical statement, I find that it has at once to be modified by the Spirit of God who can indeed break up all allegedly indissoluble states of union. This is the basis of true deliverance or exorcism: it is performed under the aegis of God, whose authority transcends any purely psychic power without in any way denying that power. God is both the Creator and the Master of the physical universe, the mental world and the psychic sphere.

We, as ignorant humans, automatically take charge of one aspect of our great world, and in so doing bring it down to our diminutive size. In this way we can deify even ourselves and our treasured possessions. When we are confronted by 'natural disasters' – floods, hurricanes, droughts and famines, such as were encountered repeatedly in the history of the Bible – we come rapidly to the conclusion that mankind acting on its own is little more than a broken reed. It is then that an almost automatic response to the unknown God breaks forth from the lips of a previously urbane, agnostic population. Such is the great variation in the attitude of unthinking humans; brusque arrogance moving rapidly to humble prayer before the Unknown God whom it hopes is still there. Those who are psychically aware are less agnostic about the personal power of the agents of good and evil. These agents have been known for generations as 'angels', which are messengers from on high, even if the message they transmit is not always pleasant or even holy. They are nevertheless the intermediaries between God and the more material creation.

It is evident that not all spiritual beings or entities, working from the psychic realm, are beneficial. Some, by their spiritual attentiveness and inner beauty, lead us closely to the Divine Presence. It is essentially those who divert our attention from the great spiritual quest whose end is the discovery and service of God – and lead us to seek instead for security, the approval of other people, and worldly rewards at the end of the day – that are pernicious, even demonic in origin. In the end, as we have already said, nobody can serve two masters.

2

The Psychic and Spiritual Fields of Experience

There was a time when people who exhibited abnormalities of behaviour, such as were at variance with the great majority of the general population, were believed to be possessed, or at least obsessed (or infested) by demonic spirits. In those days, the autonomy of the individual was far less respected than is the case nowadays; indeed it was seldom acknowledged as a fact in its own right, and the group as a whole was expected to follow a common route of belief and embrace a uniform tradition of behaviour. Therefore if a person moved sharply away from the common multitude on their own into an unusual channel of belief or action, there was a tendency to attribute this 'backsliding' to an arcane influence working from a malicious source and producing strange, possibly evil, effects. These effects might be local to the person or else involve the community as a larger unit. The personal effects tended to isolate the individual, separating them from their peer group, so that they acted independently following their belief systems. These involved their own views of the compelling mysteries of life and immortality.

If their views and the behaviour that accrued from them were apparently beneficial or at least neutral, they were left in peace or even honoured on occasions; the prophetic tradition of the Bible is an arresting case in point. But sometimes the effects seemed to have a malign influence on the person from whom they emanated, or, worse still, on those in their vicinity. This type of contact is usually a directly personal one, but some especially psychically potent people could have a more widespread influence. The essence of such a bad effect is a feeling of malaise with an awareness of a subtle interruption of one's own cognitive and emotional functions. We shall consider this matter in chapter 3.

The psychic influence we all possess and emanate as part of our personality is integral to us as individuals. It is morally neutral; like the body with its odour or the intellect with its pungency and wit, it defines and illuminates our individuality. The word 'psychic' conjures up in the imagination various occult, highly undesirable practices and phenomena including dabbling with spirits forbidden in the Scripture. This is, however, essentially the left-hand path into psychic practice, in rather the same way as physical violence hurts the body. 'Surely you know that you are God's temple, where the Spirit of God dwells' is the way St Paul puts it in 1 Corinthians 3.16, and dishonest behaviour sullies the workings and reputation of the mind. If we were to pursue this comparison, there is also a distinctly negative difference between physical and intellectual activity on the one hand and psychic activity on the other. Psychic power is far more insidious in its action than anything that is purely rational and its results are potentially far more dangerous, unless it is employed under the strict direction of the Holy Spirit. It is for this reason that the Bible repeatedly denounces trafficking in spirits (Leviticus 19.26, 31; 20.6, 27; Deuteronomy 18.10–12; Acts 8.11, 20–2).

My world-view is that of a central creative focus whom I call God, and who is a power of infinite intelligence and initiative to the extent of universal creation whose creatures can choose their own way of life. If they choose selfishly, they cause general havoc and destruction, whereas a choice of general concern blesses the whole community. The story of the Fall in Genesis 3 appears to substantiate this view, while my own experience in life as well as my reading of Scripture seem to confirm this historical perspective and the idea that selfishness leads to accidents. Evil spirits use their God-given free will selfishly and produce general mayhem or simply act out of ignorance. I do not know how, but their presence in all our lives, if left unattended, will engender increasing chaos, both personal and communal. I believe the spiritual realm is structured around God, the Divine Presence. The spiritual forces around God are both good and evil; the good bring creativity together (synthesis) while the evil tend to be separative. The forces are the angels of light and darkness, all of which emanate from God. The former transmit divine light to the creation with faith, hope and love; whereas the latter bring with them feelings of despair, distrust and self-centred concern. All this ensures that we keep alive day by day; our first duty is to keep alive until our immediate family and social tasks have been fulfilled.

The main topics of this book embrace exorcism and deliverance, psychic and spiritual fields of experience, the experience of the unquiet dead, psychic assaults, and demonic infestation including attacks on property and people. Finally, there are measures of deliverance of demonic agents and preventive measures against demonic attack.

The psychic aspect of the personality constitutes the inner core that makes us unique to those who know us as people in our own right: as something more than that vast conglomeration of humans that are collectively called 'the masses' by sociologists and politicians. If indeed we could be true to ourselves in the vast concourse of living creatures, of whom the human is the greatest in our world, we would set our stamp on God's work and play our full part in the evolution of society. Meister Eckhart remarked that God required our assistance no less than we required his. This work of transforming society under the divine direction is not forced or frenzied; on the contrary, we reveal ourselves best to others when we are relaxed; neither trying to impress anyone else nor putting up any resistance. In this degree of self-surrender to the moment at hand, we can let down our defences and enjoy the world. This includes other people with their own psychic emanations and the wider powers that impinge on us from sources beyond this mortal world.

Jesus told his disciples to seek first the kingdom of God and his justice, and all the necessary things of the world would come to them also. He told them not to worry about tomorrow, for tomorrow will take care of itself. Each day has trouble enough of its own (Matthew 6.33-4). Such trust in God's providence seems totally impractical, but in fact if we rest in him while working for the coming of the kingdom, our mental and spiritual horizons enlarge out of all previous proportions as we see how small is the space we occupy in the divine plan, and how we are cared for – once we can shift our consciousness beyond the confines of the ego to that of other people also.

And in this greater awareness we automatically divest ourselves of anxiety, in the process establishing our unique identity as finite people who bear the fruit of an immense creative impulse in the light of immortality around ourselves. This light is the Spirit of God especially illuminated and enriched by our own contribution to it.

The psychic aspect of our personality is what we begin to share with other people, in the first instance those with whom we find ourselves to be pleasantly in harmony. This is in fact the basis of friendship, which seems to descend on us like a precious gift of God. A so-called friendship that depends on sharing ideological or mental opinions and views is seldom stable and is liable, when the relationship is put under severe strain, to crack disastrously. There may be a subsequent healing but be that as it may, such a sequence of events shows both parties their lamentable lack of self-knowledge let alone their understanding of any-one else. It is hardly to be wondered at that many marriages sooner or later end in the divorce court. It is a truism that a newly married couple have to work on their marriage if it is to thrive, but in fact even before this there has to be a constant working on oneself.

Likewise, if one has to share accommodation with some-one else after having lived alone for a long time, one's eyes ought to be open to various less attractive aspects of oneself (as well as those of the other person). These unattractive personality traits centre on selfishness in its various insidi-ous manifestations, especially that one's own requirements should be met as promptly as possible. As the process of self-revelation is assimilated, so one's eye is cast more and more accusingly on one's own inherent self-centredness; after much heart-searching and inner humiliation one may increase immeasurably in spiritual strength. This process follows a deeper psychic contact with numerous other people whom one learns to respect and love for what they are as people in their own right. It is in this fashion that psychic expansion occurs on a basically human level.

But as this process continues, so does the power of God reveal itself more and more. This is shown by a great con-cern and love not only between two people but also among a considerable community with diverse mundane interests. I suspect that this process fertilized the lives of Jesus' earliest disciples as recorded in the opening chapters of the Acts of the Apostles. In this example a charismatic figure, indeed the Godhead in human revelation, brought the apostles together in an amazing communal synthesis: they never surrendered their identity while at the same time growing into a human formation that completely dwarfed their previous stature. In this amazing phenomenon we see psy-chic union attaining its apogee through the work of the Holy Spirit, so that the humans themselves begin to live, at least for a period, on the spiritual plane.

If we consider the means of human relationship, we

begin to share ourselves with other people by bodily union, of which sexual intercourse is simply one form, albeit a very intimate one. It can become a instrument of hatred just as easily as one of affection. If our sharing is more profound we proceed to communicate our thoughts and ideas to other people intellectually also, but here again there is a variable degree of commitment and withdrawal. When we are able to trust ourselves more profoundly, we can give and receive equally fully so that our communication can move beyond physical and mental barriers. At this point we begin to know the other person – and many other matters also – by direct intuition, which has been described by C. G. Jung as communication by means of the unconscious. This, I believe, is how we communicate psychically, and how we are put in contact with sources of the past and future that are outside rational knowledge.

The connecting link between these three ways of human relationship is the fourth, which is the presence of God, the Holy Spirit. While we are open and obedient to this perfectly spiritual influence it is important to understand that we will still have to bear 'the slings and arrows of outrageous fortune', as Shakespeare puts it in *Hamlet* 3. 3. 59 in the famous soliloquy. Obedience to the good does not exempt us from savage attacks by the evil, and many may be killed in age-old holocausts. But life is something more than temporal satisfaction; it is nothing less than the growth of the person into the stature of the perfect individual as seen most majestically in the person of Christ. Did not Jesus tell his disciples, 'In the world you will have suffering. But take heart! I have conquered the world' (John 16.33)? Dame Julian of Norwich was told much the same over thirteen hundred years later: 'He did not say you will not have a difficult time, you will never bear severe strain, you will never feel severe discomfort. But he *did* say you will never be overcome' (Revelation 68). The uncomfortable truth is that we do grow through suffering, but the end of the process is a renewed person able to contribute to the welfare of the whole community in a new way.

Returning once more to the theme that opened this chapter – that people whose belief systems or behaviour patterns were distinctly different from those of the majority of their peers were believed to be subject to the influence of evil, or at least alien entities – the current attitude is that these people are mentally ill and in need of specialized psychiatric help. Psychic influences from afar are no longer a tenable premise except among very unusual practitioners, for nearly all mental disturbance is recognized as being secondary to cerebral disturbance on the one hand and the effects of past experience on the present attitude of the person (producing various adverse emotional states) on the other. This point of view is certainly much more convenient than invoking far less substantial psychical, or paranormal, and spiritual categories of classification. But can they be summarily disregarded without doing injustice to the human personality as a whole and our own experience in particular? In the end we have to make our own judgement, moving between the two polarities of personal prejudice and superstition on the one hand and intellectual assurance with its arrogance on the other. Ultimately experience is our only teacher – we can only judge the skill of a professional teacher by the effect the person has upon our inner intuition of truth (Matthew 7.28–9) – but it must be correlated by being compared with the experience of other people. This point of reference is put into a scientific framework by the collection of data and noting whether they correspond with each other. If a group of people claiming roughly comparable experiences that are quite unusual in quality are nevertheless able to communicate with each other and the remainder of the community, it is reasonable to deduce that they are mentally healthy to the extent of being of special use to the community. If, on the other hand, their experiences, whether misinterpreted or true, lead them to overestimate their own qualities and

16

denigrate those of other people, then they are in a dangerous state of psychic inflation and need urgent deliverance from what is invading them.

If we can begin to perceive the ministry of deliverance in these terms, we are coming to something thoroughly practical and no longer merely couched in medieval superstition. The condition of individual psychic inflation, often combined with a tendency to denigrate the powers of other people, can easily proceed to an 'obsessional belief system', in which a considerable number of people may be involved. The obsessional belief system can assume a quasi-physical character, traditionally and loosely called a 'ghost', but this can usually be exorcised by a capable minister of deliverance quite easily, once the people involved are appraised of the situation and move beyond addictive fascination to the lower psychic levels of communication. I am incidentally not implying that all obsessional systems are primarily self-induced. I have little doubt that many impinge on and invade the person from outside their immediate psychic proximity. But they would produce a far less baneful effect on a psychically healthy, strong person, more able to cope with their own personal problems and those of people who relate closely to them. What I am saying was put far more succinctly and cogently by St Paul to his Ephesian disciples. 'Speak the truth to each other, for we belong to one another' (Ephesians 4.25). Thoughts on a similar theme were written by John Donne in his *Devotions*. Good examples are, 'No man is an Island, entire of it self'; 'Any man's death diminishes me, because I am involved in Mankind; and therefore never send to know for whom the bell tolls; it tolls for thee'; 'But I do nothing upon my self, and yet I am mine own *Executioner.*'

In our brief life on earth we all have much to learn. I know one thing only; love overcomes all things whereas fear leads to hatred, which is a monstrously destructive emotion, never so dreadful as when it has a religious basis. This fear can easily work through psychic phenomena, and the hatred that is stirred up can set up a terrible chain reaction. Many of the most awful deeds in human history have been brought about by psychical activities devoid of a spiritual basis. But when God is truly in control, his presence is shown by a selfless concern for one's neighbour, who, in the teaching of Jesus, includes everyone (Luke 10.29-37).

A last thought is one of value judgements. The spiritual leads us in our personal quest to the knowledge of God, while the psychical brings us closer together both as people and as living forces in our world. The intellectual helps us to develop our personal gifts and potentialities for our own benefit and that of others also, while the physical gives us a body to use for earthly life moment by moment. It is through the physical body that we live, at least temporarily in our world, where we gain so much experience for our onward trail. Therefore although the spiritual level may be the highest of the four, it is in no way the most important. All that God has given us is equally valuable and important.

I must add a final caveat: this is a description of my way of working, not a blueprint for others to follow, even if it challenges all of my readers to a greater degree of spiritual discipline, whether they are practising a deliverance ministry or not.

3

Disturbances due to Psychic Assaults

As has already been stated, there are some people who appear to be preternaturally aware of the emotional atmosphere of a locality; they can immediately recognize a disturbance in a room in their home which they know well enough through past familiarity, but at the present time simply feels cold and alien. This sensitivity is clearly essentially subjective, and both strangers and some friends who know the environment quite well may be unaware of anything unusual. On the other hand, a visitor with little prior knowledge of the area may quickly sense something wrong with the atmosphere, sufficient on occasions to produce a distinct feeling of depression. Sometimes strange physical phenomena may also occur, such as the displacement of objects from their customary situations to locations where they may suddenly appear after a variable period of complete absence. In such circumstances it may well be that the psychic energy that emanates from the person (or people) works to reinforce a psychically charged atmosphere or object.

Sometimes the atmosphere has been a notorious feature of the locality for a long time; sometimes it has descended dramatically like an autumnal fog. The analogy with a fog which encloses one inescapably can be quite apt, for its intensity may dull the senses as well as depressing the awareness of light and humour that lies very close to the joy of living. The nature of this negative feeling is obscure to the intellectual type of observer who may with irritation dismiss the whole matter as 'ideas' in the minds of people with too little work to do, but these 'ideas', if disregarded, may form the basis of a depressive illness. The question immediately follows: has the phenomenon come in as a reaction to a period of depression afflicting someone in the environment, or was the phenomenon the spark that set off the depression in an especially sensitive person? In the majority of cases that I have encountered, the human agent has been the primary target of attack, and in their turn has added to the general psychic mêlée.

It is helpful right at the start of this discussion to note that the clearance of malign psychic atmosphere is not synonymous with exorcism or deliverance. In the latter circumstance we believe that an actual tangible entity is haunting a particular locality and causing a disturbance, because it is acting blindly and seeking for its release, or less frequently desiring to frighten or confuse its victim. The discarnate entity should be put into the care of God, not cast out of its present situation into the terrible wrath of providence, which is conspicuously lacking in even elementary love. The battle that would ensue would have an inevitably favourable outcome, but the havoc caused might be of extreme destructiveness. But what we are at present considering is not the removal or exorcism of an invading entity, but merely the cleansing of an unwholesome atmosphere.

A good analogy would be a public house inundated with cigarette smoke or the fumes of liquor coming from the bottles opened by the attendant. Psychical unwholesomeness follows the presence of emotionally disturbed people in a locality, and sensitive individuals can be aware of undercurrents of sadness, fear, anger or any other negative emotion very quickly. They may not know the cause of the disturbance, but of its presence they have no doubt. In a number of well-recorded cases it has been established that a violent death occurred in the same house, even the same room, on a previous occasion. This type of sequence has occurred too frequently to be dismissed merely as coincidence. On the other hand, a room that has been the scene of great rejoicing in the past also tends to retain an atmosphere of happiness and celebration. As I have already stated all this sensitivity would verge on the ridiculous, but before we cast it all out as primitive superstition, let us compare the situation with that of a highly musical person who might go out of their way to hear a noted performer while an equally intelligent person might be deaf to the arts generally, believing them to serve no useful function in the advancement of human knowledge or endeavour. In the immediate period there would probably be no meeting of the two minds at all; one could only hope that in due course the artistically illiterate person would have their aesthetic and emotional ears and eyes opened to appreciate the spiritual grandeur of great music and art, and to be transformed by it.

The reverse situation is barely conceivable. Physically and intellectually we function as separate units, often extremely selfish ones, but when we enter into the collective experience of humanity as evidenced in the inspiration of the greatest art, we lose ourselves in order to find our true being which goes far beyond personal preference and enjoyment to include the whole of creation. It is when we lose our sense of separation in the wonder of the present scene that we can move beyond even an attachment to the greatest art to the divine essence on which the beautiful, the true and the good are eternally fixed. All that we can comprehend with the senses has its own limitations; all that we can grasp psychically has, as it were, frayed edges as one part merges into the other; but what we encounter spiritually changes us as people. The term 'deification' is used by the Eastern Orthodox Church to describe the inner change that follows the influx of the Holy Spirit into the chastened soul. A completely renewed person emerges as the power of the Holy Spirit acts psychically to cleanse the soul and the body.

From this consideration of individual psychic malaise and its treatment, it seems clear that the work of the Holy Spirit is of paramount importance not only in clearing away noxious psychic miasmas but also in replacing them with a wholesome atmosphere of peace, hope and joy. The Holy Spirit can be identified with the healing presence of God, bringing clear sight into a situation of chaos so that one can at last be able to discern the problem clearly without interference from other people, emotional attitudes, and all dark psychic backgrounds with menacingly evil emanations. The emanations arise from the emotions of people still alive, to which are added the negative feelings of those departed from this mortal framework. In this respect it is a wise dictum that what we are now we shall continue to be in the future, at least until we strive to change our attitudes and ways.

I personally believe that we carry on with us our basic emotional attitudes and prejudices even after the death of the physical body, an acceptance of probable fact articulated by many psychic types of people. If this is true, then it is all too probable that we, or more precisely our souls, continue in a psychic flux between earth and the afterlife, a sort of purgatorial zone, until we are able to confront the course of our past life with courage and honesty. Then we may know fully the meaning of forgiveness as a new sheet is opened in the book of our lives, and the guilt and regrets of the past are wiped away as remnants of a past when we were still in the school of life.

It follows from this observation that the closer we are to God in assiduous prayer, the more protected we are from psychic assaults from invidious environments. No one can be totally protected, nor should we aim at such total protection – as we noted in the first chapter, it is through spiritual conflict that we grow in stature as people – but if we play our part nobly we shall not be vanquished but, on the contrary, be justly rewarded with the spiritual and psychical strength that comes from the Divine Source. The value of playing our part in the various problems and tragedies that beset our little world is that it brings us closer to our human compatriots to the extent that we may enter directly into their feelings and know what is going on in their hearts. An astute psychologist can project their personality into the object of contemplation, so fully comprehending it. This power of personal rapport is called empathy. The object is nearly always a fellow human, and when the inner fields of the person can be comprehended, an attempt can be made to relate to the individual to relieve them of their problem. The work of empathy has a strong psychic basis, but it also involves emotional sympathy and intellectual acuity. Some experienced medical practitioners have a built-in psychic reserve that warns them that a particular patient whose clinical history may not differ very much from the norm is in particular danger of death.

It should be noted that a demonic spirit is complete in its form even when it reveals its malevolence by being misplaced, for instance in human company rather than by staying aloof. The way those symptoms differ from those of spiritual dryness is distinguished by their response to deliverance. Once the invading spirit is sent back to God's care, the symptoms rapidly resolve. The great majority of people who have rejected their faith have done so for many other considerations, such as disillusionment, general depression, or personal dislike of ministers who had previously visited them and left an atmosphere of coldness behind them.

I believe that disturbances in the psychic atmosphere are invariably due to hostile emotions from people who have or have had some connection with the locality. A classical example of this hostile response is the familiar poltergeist, the German for 'playful spirit'. It shows itself in overt physical phenomena in the ambience of an adolescent who usually has quite severe emotional problems. The age of the person is usually one at which sexual arousal is proceeding *pari passu* with genital development, and the person is not in complete control of their emotions. Indeed, they may be quite ignorant about the full nature of sexuality, even in our very permissive society. As a result of this parental negligence the youngster is generally unhappy and maladjusted. There is nearly always an emotional problem with someone else, or more than one person, of about the same age group. In my own experience the person involved can also be of adult age or even elderly. The connecting feature seems to be the emotional state of the person rather than the age.

In one of the most memorable occasions of this type of phenomenon, I was called on to investigate strange paranormal events occurring in a home for underprivileged children. It was shown to me that the problem was one of poltergeist activity (this 'showing' is a response to deep prayer, as I shall describe in chapter 9), and that the 'treatment' (to use a medical analogy) was a period of equally deep prayer with the staff, a blessing of the premises, and, most important of all, a general discussion with the staff of both the nature of the disturbance and the way of dealing with it. There is in fact no stereotyped approach to treating a poltergeist apart from dealing with the emotional problems besetting its victim. While that individual is unhappy and discontented the chances are sure that the disturbances will recur. I found that in this particular case the children were too strictly controlled despite the loving care bestowed on them and that some of them were previously mentally disturbed. When subsequently the control was sensibly loosened, the relaxed atmosphere proved conducive to a fairly rapid disappearance of the very unpleasant psychic phenomena.

It is especially important in this type of case not to practise any type of exorcism, because there is rarely anything to 'cast out' other than the unpleasant atmosphere and the fear of the people in the vicinity. All these are best dealt with by a simple but heartfelt blessing, together with the laying-on of hands. The significance of this gesture is debatable. I believe that it has direct healing power which is mediated psychically, for numerous 'spiritual healers' seem to emit a directly healing influence by this means. Again all this can be ascribed to mere suggestion, but anyone who has received this type of treatment is frequently aware of intense heat emanating from the practitioner's hands. This heat was my own personal introduction to the ministry of healing. One thing is certain: it is stronger than the normal body temperature. I believe that this is one of a number of phenomena that form a connection between the physical and psychical fields of activity.

This thought brings us to consider poltergeist activity more precisely: the type of person most likely to be afflicted has been described, but what actually happens in their vicinity? The phenomena are of physical type: the unexplained movement of objects which may disappear unaccountably for a variable period of time and then reappear just as unexpectedly and quite often in their customary site; unexplained switching on and off of lights; unusual sounds like the heavy tread of footsteps outside the premises and of sufficient intensity as to mimic an approaching intruder; the turning on of taps and their subsequent tightening again. But can we explain this strange assembly? We have to admit that psychical phenomena cannot be explained scientifically with such certainty that everybody agrees about their very existence, let alone their mechanism. This uncertainty is related to their unpredictability; since the essence of scientific research is the repeatability of the phenomena. Psychical research, at least at the present time, fails to qualify as a scientific discipline. Poltergeist activity cannot be produced at will, as can the physical phenomena associated with scientific research.

My own view is that psychic energy might be converted into physical energy, and when conditions were right might express itself in a manifest fashion. The right conditions might be those of harmonization of the particular psychic energies of the person with those of the surrounding environment. When the two articulated simultaneously it could be that a physical manifestation might occur. The apparent purposelessness of poltergeist activity and its anonymous nature do not suggest a personal mischievous source from afar causing the trouble. It is, of course, possible that a mischievous source might harness a poltergeist for its own unpleasant purposes, but on the whole it is wiser to employ Occam's razor: the use of the fewest assumptions in explaining a thing. Having said this quite categorically, one must also note that in biological systems, which include disease processes, it is common for a number of different factors to work together, but nearly always one takes precedence over the others.

I do not believe that the poltergeist is necessarily malign in intent any more than a severe storm has a diabolical origin. But the alarm it may occasion in people – it often occurs in a group living closely together – can be quite considerable. It may be of value in obliging people to look more deeply into their spiritual life, even to the extent of evaluating their past in the light of possible future developments.

4

Problems Relating to the
Unquiet Dead

———◦◦◦◦◦◦◦———

Let it be admitted at once that no one knows with certainty whether we survive death. The agnostic would laugh the suggestion out of court since to them consciousness resides in the brain, and when this has undergone the irreversible changes associated with death all that remains is a quickly rotting corpse. People with a more spiritual view of existence seem to have much less difficulty with the concept of survival and immortality of the essence of a person, which is traditionally called the soul, or the true self. Sceptics tend to attribute this conviction to the refusal of the person to face the fact of their finitude; and indeed the thought of a total and final obliteration of consciousness can remain a terrible threat to all but the most lion-hearted people, no matter how dogmatically they may assert their belief in some sort of afterlife. The belief in the existence of an after-life state is built into human consciousness and forms part of the credal statements of many religions, starting from antiquity and persisting to the present time. A belief as firm as this deserves some analysis.

There is first of all the integrity of the individual personality so that each of us is unique in their own right and has an equally unique contribution to make to the whole. Life is a system of individual growth, starting with the infant with a mind no larger than its body but developing into an organism who can think, feel and act creatively. This growth and creative action is not simply an isolated personal phenomenon, but is related to the whole community so that our life is far greater than our own perception of it. When we die the contribution does not disappear, but on the contrary lives on in the lives of those whom we knew while in our mortal bodies. But what exactly lives on? It is our psychic presence that is the basis of the freshness of joyful memory; but in the same way it can cast a cloud of darkness when it is distraught and maladjusted. The freshness of our psychic presence is related to its positive work in the world, primarily in the here and now but in a more universal way among all creatures living and dead in the vale of immortality. A third reason that makes us believe most strongly in a life beyond death is the question of the growth of the personality into realms of understanding far beyond anything we could imagine in terms of conditions on an earthly plane.

Much of our lives here are necessarily confined to the squalor of the earth around us. What we make of the earth speaks volumes about ourselves. Some sully it with their psychic residues of greed, hatred and dishonesty. Others enrich it with the psychic grace of good deeds, caring for the world (the reverence for life stressed years ago by Albert Schweitzer), and having an attitude of generosity towards one's fellow creatures – no matter how much they may differ from oneself in lifestyle, religious belief and practice, to say nothing of such basic, irreversible matters as race, sex and family background. Nor can our response to the living conditions of others be ignored, especially the aged, the mentally ill, and those who have borne the burden of the world's cruelty through the horrors of persecution, of which our own century has been so terrible a witness.

If this is the only life, and physical death overtakes us all inevitably and without any redress, the quality of our life here becomes irrelevant. St Paul parodies it thus, 'Let us eat and drink, for tomorrow we die' (1 Corinthians 15.32). No doubt the 'spiritual person' will at once retort that one should not be living virtuously now with an eye to benefits in the hereafter, and this is very true. But in fact the type of person who lives in this attitude of submerged spiritual self-interest – in truth a very unpleasant hypocritical egoism – is nowhere near God or anything approaching heavenly grace. They are immersed in the baleful pleasures of self-concern to the virtual exclusion of any deep relationship with their fellow humans, and the end of their life is increasing exclusion from the hearts and souls of other people. This fact is made more clear to them as they lie dying, and especially after their essence, the soul, drifts away from the earth it once knew so well in attachment with the physical body, which is now an expendable remnant. Of all this I personally have no doubt through my own gift of clairvoyance, which may be defined as a capacity of perceiving, as if by seeing, what is happening or exists out of sight. (A related capacity of perceiving, as if by hearing, is known as clairaudience; neither of these capacities is rare as occasional phenomena in the experience of many people, but their occurrence is at best sporadic and cannot be summarily commanded.)

In this respect we remember what Jesus said during the nocturnal visit of Nicodemus: 'The wind blows where it wills; you can hear the sound of it but you do not know where it comes from or where it is going. So it is with everyone who is born from the Spirit' (John 3.8). Psychical gifts are basically personal phenomena, whereas spiritual gifts ennoble the whole person, in the course of which there is a refinement of the innate psychic sensitivity of the individual so that they become acutely sensitive to vast ranges of existence quite remote from the awareness of their peers. It is this type of psychic sensitivity that is especially valuable, but it is under the aegis of the Holy Spirit and a pure gift of God.

People who claim that they can communicate at will with other modalities of existence beyond earthly realms should be treated with the greatest agnosticism and also some degree of healthy caution if the possibility of magic comes across one's awareness. The undifferentiated psychic realm is far closer to the demonic than the divine. Only a deeply spiritual person, one steeped in prayer, can enter the psychic realm with some degree of safety, and here the motive is all important. Is the penetration of psychic awareness for the benefit of a person or people in special danger or need, or is it a purely selfish action with power or prestige as its basis? Only a life of constant prayer can differentiate between these two motives, because our unaided will and conscience is childishly naive rather than frankly evil in intent.

'The spirit is willing, but the flesh is weak' (Matthew 26.41), was Jesus' diagnosis of the human spiritual condition, and until the flesh, which is basic human nature, is cleansed, regenerated and resurrected, people will continue to travel the well-worn path of selfishness. This leads to an almost intolerable isolation on 'the other side of death', as one of my most psychologically erudite friends, a psychotherapist who had studied with Jung himself, so felicitously put it. This person has long been dead, but his soul was for a long time not at peace despite his great metaphysical knowledge. The reason for this sad state of affairs – despite his excellent work as a teacher as well as a therapist – was due to a brilliant intellect. He tended to look down on most other people, including his fellow therapists. Two hundred years ago Mozart behaved similarly and suffered accordingly except that in his case he became rapidly impoverished and was buried in a large communal grave, whereas my friend was extremely well off financially though terrified about the financial situation of the world he was soon to leave. His gloom seemed to us to be merely a negative reaction to his impending death (despite his oft-declared belief in the survival of the personality after the death of the body), but in fact there was a very great financial recession some months after his death. It is evident that this psychically and psychologically gifted man was afforded a shaft of precognition, which may be defined as a supernatural foreknowledge of events that are outside the bounds of received information. (The reverse condition, retrocognition, is considerably more common; it is the supernatural knowledge of events that occurred in the past in a locality that were outside the bounds of received knowledge. Examples were noted in chapter 3 of people who had sensed unpleasant atmospheres in rooms and homes where there had been enacted tragedies or sordid crimes in the past.)

It has been shown to me by the gift of clairvoyance that when a person dies the physical 'I', recognized only a small time before, has dissolved, and the essence of the person, the soul, is laid bare. There is a very rapid confrontation of their past; the protective function of the body has been irrevocably removed, and now the inner nature is stripped of all illusions related to worldly position or temporal success. Time is gradually swallowed up into eternity just as space now expands into infinity. The familiar doxology says it all much more eloquently, 'As it was in the beginning, is now, and ever shall be, world without end'. The world we at present inhabit is a mere speck on the horizon of eternity, but its very finiteness is exactly what we require for our growth from selfish, unaware children to mature, responsible adults.

The key process that moves us along the path of growth from unaware childhood to full adult stature is service to our fellow creatures, a service that becomes healthy and positively useful only when one gains insight into one's own character. The more suffering we are obliged to undergo as a result of our selfishness the wiser we become, the more acute do our sensitivities to the needs of others reveal themselves to be, and the more generally does the centre of our concern move from the personal microcosm to the infinitely greater world around us, which, as I have already indicated, is a very limited field of eternity also. This is the very meaning of our incarnation, and on its fruits depend the deeper circumstances of our death and the events that succeed it. The more our general attitude towards our fellow humans expands and becomes the core of our concern, in other words, the more that love dominates our lives on earth, and the more easily does the soul become detached from the body when it dies. If the life of the person has not been especially edifying when they were in the living state, the attachment to mundane things persists after death, and on occasion distinct phenomena may reveal themselves to psychically sensitive people.

Usually one can sense a soul in distress by its sudden, completely unexpected contact with the higher reaches of the mind – in other words, from the height of the conscious level of awareness. This is no emotional sensation, but rather a direct, sometimes almost imperious, message for help. The helper must be someone with strong psychic sensitivity but also with the capacity to afford help. Usually the problem is one of guilt for a misdemeanour committed in the past life of the person, and it may vary from a very nasty crime to a quite venial sin which has long troubled the conscience of the individual but has almost equally long been forgotten, or certainly forgiven, by the other person. 'There is no fear in love; but perfect love casts out fear' (1 John 4.18); this injunction shows the way towards dealing with this type of unquiet, or earthbound, spirit of a dead person.

Therefore one prays first to God using the Lord's Prayer and the Collect for the Nineteenth Sunday after Trinity: 'O God, forasmuch as without thee we are not able to please thee; Mercifully grant, that thy Holy Spirit may in all things direct and rule our hearts; through Jesus Christ our Lord. Amen.' After this comes a few minutes' completely silent contemplation followed by another few minutes' equally silent prayer to God. Then the spirit of the deceased person is addressed in terms of love and consolation in which the eternal forgiveness of God is emphasized, provided there is genuine repentance on the part of the offender. In the post-mortem state this is far more certain to be attained than when the individual was still alive, for by this time there will have been a general assessment of his or her life on earth and a burning desire to amend their ways in the future. The procedure ends by pronouncing the words of an absolution from the liturgy of a particular religious tradition. These words have to be said with the intent uttered by the priest over a living penitent, and it is far better if a priest absolves an unquiet dead person. But, as I have already said, this is no play-acting sequence, and should be performed only by a psychically aware person or at least one sympathetic to the ideas that I discussed above.

It should be emphasized that a psychically sensitive person could just as easily be unordained as a minister of any Christian (or, for that matter, any other) denomination. It would be ungracious to God to reject help from any quarter as long as it is spiritually pure and detached from material motive. The cruelties committed in the name of religion cannot make any faith *ipso facto* sacrosanct. Therefore an irreligious person, but one who was deeply spiritual in their approach and actions to their neighbour, could be as helpful in dealing with an unquiet spirit as one who was quite bigoted and intolerant. I accept the authority of holy orders, but how these are used depends on the character of the minister. The question depends on the relationship between spirituality and religion. The former is a person's relationship with God and their neighbour, so that if these two are radiant, the individual is deeply spiritual no matter what faith they may profess. By contrast, religion is a system of belief that should lead to a spiritual way of life. Religion, except in the hands of deeply spiritual people, cannot help becoming divisive. It is little surprise that many highly intelligent people discard religion categorically, but their guidepost to civilized living is undermined in the process. In the end they are obliged to reinstate some sort of religion in their lives, but the experience of fanatical intolerance followed by belligerent agnosticism may, one hopes, lead to a more moderate, intelligent type of faith that increases their spiritual potential.

The matter of psychically sensitive people who claim to have communication with the spirits of the dead is a very

contentious issue. These people are called 'mediums', especially by hostile witnesses, but 'sensitives' by those who are
more detached in their approach. I have, as I already noted,
little doubt that some people have a gift of psychic awareness, but it cannot be called to order despite the claims of
some psychics. Furthermore, there is no guarantee of the
integrity of their communicators, for some are not what they
seem and may well be demonic in character. It is for these
reasons that lay psychics are seldom used by professional
ministers of religion.

I personally had the rare privilege of working closely
with a gifted psychic who was a convinced Christian of
Anglo-Catholic sympathies. We worked for twelve years
over the telephone at about 10.30 p.m. each evening, and
we were progressively trained for work first of all by being
shown how to release dead war criminals and other mis-
creants from the hell in which they had placed themselves
by the method I have already outlined. The psychic
component of this partnership (I provided a lesser gift of
sensitivity) was a lady in her early eighties called Geraldine
('Geral') whom everybody believed was finished as a working
force and fit only for imminent death. However, our work
progressed apace, and she gained measurably in health and
strength. Her only impediment was severe deafness, but
this was much less severe over the telephone. After we had
done some work for war criminals and a Chinese group
who required releasing from the imprisonment of the lower
reaches of the afterlife, we were 'certified ready', I believe
by God, to help individuals who had recently died and
whose souls were still earthbound. In some cases they had
been dead for some longer time, even several years. When
we had contacted the unfortunate individual entities (a
useful word to denote an earthbound spirit) I was sometimes
instructed simply to give absolution. On other occasions it
was clear that the entity was in a state of confusion, not
knowing let alone understanding its present disposition in
the life eternal. It was my special work to explain matters
to the entity, telling it where it was in its present situated,

and how important it was that it should move forthwith from its earthbound situation, where it could cause considerable confusion among those living in the location, both emotionally and by producing poltergeist-like phenomena. In my experience I had to address the entity firmly but kindly, explaining the present circumstances clearly and indicating how much happier it would be if it were to quit the earthbound plane and move to that place in the life eternal which God has prepared for its reception and healing.

There are two basic causes for an entity to remain earthbound: obstinacy and extreme ignorance of the present circumstances, to which may be added a feeling of severe guilt. In these circumstances, I would explain the situation, persuading the entity to quit its present place of domicile and proceed to the place in the life beyond death which God has prepared for its reception and healing. Above all, I encourage this process with a promise of God's loving care when a positive move has been made to leave the earthbound plane and proceed from the darkness of the present to the light surrounding it once its sight has been opened to the greater truth of the present situation. This light is the power of the Holy Spirit, remembering the dictum of 1 John 1.5, 'God is light, and in him there is no darkness at all.'

When I address the entity I prefer not to use its earthly Christian name, but rather attune myself to its eternal character, but others of a less mystical bent might prefer to be more specific in naming the entity. In fact when we deal with matters that transcend the grave, we are especially wise to be guided by sources above our normal consciousness. The Anglican liturgy speaks of angels and archangels and all the company of heaven – an angel being a special messenger of God's grace. I always enquire from above whether there is a focus of guilt clouding the conscience of the entity and preventing its release from its present earthbound situation, and if such guilt is present, I enquire from God whether it is right and proper that I should say the words of absolution. In some cases there is no true conversion; the entity wants release but entertains no really positive change of mind, in which case it has to be left to follow its own way. In this respect this course of action differs from the expulsion of a demonic (evil) spirit, which must be delivered into God's care whether it agrees or not. It is very infrequent, at least in my experience, for an unquiet spirit to resist being transferred from its earth-bound situation to the freedom of the heavenly planes where God's love remains the only reality. As I have already indicated, ignorance and fear based on guilt for past actions while the spirit was still incarnate are the two causes for holding the spirit back.

What will happen to most of us when we have 'shuffled off this mortal coil', as Shakespeare puts it so memorably in Hamlet's immortal soliloquy (1. 3. 79)? From what has been shown to me, most of us, whose lives have been reasonably disposed to our fellows, without any taint of cruelty on the one hand or any aura of sanctity on the other, will find ourselves in a distinctly recognizable environment on the other side of death. Once we have become acclimatized to the discarnate state, we will find that our movements have the speed of thought and that our range of awareness is immeasurably greater than it was while we were limited to an earthly body. The whole panorama of our earthly life is unravelled before us, in a way well described in the now quite familiar near-death experience. Once all this information has been assimilated, the soul can evaluate the person's earthly life fairly accurately, without either blaming circumstances for its native weaknesses or cringing in shame because of past errors.

None of us is perfect, thank God, for if we were we would be almost impossible to live with because of our self-satisfied judgementalism. No wonder Jesus advises us not to judge lest we should bear the pain of retributory judgement (Matthew 7.1). The essence of holy living is not abiding by a code of rules, but giving of oneself according to the demands of common sense to those who require our assistance. If one overdoes the giving one will soon fall by the wayside of ill health, and end up by being a considerable burden on one's neighbours. If, on the other hand, we do not give what we can reasonably be expected to provide through selfishness and meanness, we lay up for ourselves a harvest of contempt and ill will where there might have been friendship and cooperation. In the afterlife this aversion of others to ourselves cannot be easily concealed, and a painful course of good manners may be in store for us before we can take our allotted place in the work of character building ahead of us.

The key word in all relationships is forgiveness. We have to forgive others who have wronged us while striving and praying to be forgiven by others whom we may wittingly or unwittingly have wronged. None of this can be done except in the presence of God, whose very nature is love: 'We love because he loved us first' (see 1 John 4.10). There are two basic Christian views of the life of the world to come: the traditional Catholic view of a gradation of existence from hell through purgatory to heaven as outlined by Dante in the *Divine Comedy*, and the opposing rigorous Protestant view of the die irrevocably cast at the moment of death, so that the undeserving person is committed to eternal hell, whereas the 'saved' individual goes straight to heaven. 'Salvation' in this unremitting scheme includes holding the right sectarian views just as much as leading the good life. Therefore those with religious beliefs other than Christianity can expect damnation when they die. This is a most terrible doctrine when some of the cruellest actions have been committed by Christians – many of whom supported Hitler's holocaust in our own century, to give a single example among countless others. Where the medieval Catholic view swerved dangerously was in making money out of the fears of the surviving relatives of the deceased who might be languishing in purgatory. These survivors prayed fervently for their loved ones – something I do each day for the many people I too remember from my association with them when I knew them as earthly companions, friends and clients. The Church, however, promised remission of temporal punishment still due for sins even after sacramental absolution, a promise made even more certain by the payment of money to the Church. This system of 'indulgences', as they were called, led inevitably to abuses and also to powerful superstition, and was the immediate inflammatory cause of the Reformation, which, at least in various extreme sects, denied the way open to the sinner, as we have already recounted. Therefore prayers for the dead were completely out of place: the 'saved' did not require them, while the damned were beyond the influence of any prayer. Humans are never so happy as when they can act with reckless abandon; throwing the baby out with the bathwater is a usual way of describing such action.

It seems worthwhile entertaining some speculations about the way forward for the distinctly quiet dead – those who have made their peace with our world and are now ready for distinct forward movement. It must be admitted that nobody knows the answer to this enigma, but certain thoughts come closely to mind. The type of heaven visualized in many religions is not only incredible but also almost intolerably boring – rather like a pleasant residential home for upper-class gentry with little to offer in the way of intellectual or spiritual stimulus. Such a condition is really close to true death, and is actually quite horrifying when one considers it entirely frankly in a state of detachment. All real living is meeting, says the Jewish sage, Martin Buber. Therefore I would expect communication on a very elevating level in the life of the world to come. Life is also growth, a product of meeting and the exchange of information on the deepest levels of experience. This deepest exchange of our own essence is the meaning of love. No wonder that there is no fear in love; but perfect love casts out fear (1 John 4.18).

But once this information has been exchanged I would

38

expect the person to continue their onward trail in order to serve the world and thereby grow even further in understanding and sanctity. We learn by suffering much more than by contentment; the cross is the symbol of what I am speaking about, and only when we too can take up our own particular cross in emulation of our Master can we enter the unitary consciousness of heaven in the company of the blessed ones. It is here that the Divine Presence is known and a peace beyond understanding savoured. This state of beatitude does not remain indefinitely, for the entity is destined to grow in darker regions by descending to a distinctly lower level of being for more training in the life of the spirit. Where this place of training might be one obviously does not know, but one possibility is a return to the earth. This is called reincarnation, which the great religions of the East – Hinduism and Buddhism – fully accept, whereas their Western counterparts – Judaism, Christianity and Islam – equally vigorously reject it; though there are individual exceptions also, for instance Shi'ite Islam.

There is some objective evidence that the belief may have substance, inasmuch as very small children may claim memories of a past life before their birth, which could not possibly have been known to them as they were neither living in the locality nor had the capacity to read at that early age. Their parents, when investigated by research workers, were equally ignorant of these long past matters. It is just possible that the children's memories are significant, but agnostics may ascribe them to a subtle priming by their parents who were less ignorant than they purported to be. Most of these cases have been reported in countries where there is a strong acceptance of rebirth. Hypnotic regression techniques can be quite startling in what they evoke, but where do the data arise: from the adult who claims the memories, the hypnotherapist, or some indifferent psychical source like a deceased entity during a spiritualistic seance? Not many parapsychologists are impressed with the findings of hypnotic regression, fascinating though some may be.

I personally am sympathetic to the concept of rebirth, of which reincarnation might be a possibility, because this earth is a particularly fine training ground for character development. If we have failed on the first occasion, it might well be that we are sent back for further work and experience. I cannot visualize a person of fine character reincarnating except if they are sent back by God on a special errand of mercy, perhaps similar to the mechanism of the incarnation, albeit on a vastly smaller scale. I have alluded to spiritualistic communication. Few people outside that field are very sympathetic, because, as in the case of hypnotherapy conjuring up past lives, one does not know the veracity of the medium's 'guide' or 'control' – a spirit who allegedly puts the medium in communication with the deceased entity. Spiritualism, little more than a century old, has some startling cases in which reliable mediums of irreproachable veracity have brought forth apparently accurate evidence of the spirit of the entity still in communication with those who knew the person when he or she was still alive in the flesh. But the number of such mediums is very small indeed – actually only three have been encountered in Britain and the USA over the last century, and none have appeared for well over fifty years – and so we all wait for the new genius to appear. The sporadic nature of psychic communication and its variable accuracy, to say nothing of the honesty of the medium (for the whole area of professional mediumship is a minefield of fraud) makes the practice of spiritualism of limited importance in releasing the unquiet dead. But I could visualize a priest working with a deeply Christian medium, as I did with my dear friend Geral, who died at the age of ninety-three some four years ago. She would never have called herself a medium, and had no time at all for spiritualists or the practice of spiritualism. It was the murky nature of so much mediumship that put her off from identifying herself with spiritualism.

5

The Principles of Demonic Infestation

——————

Demonic attack plays a significant part in the Bible. A particularly well-known reference is encountered in the Compline exhortation, 'Be on the alert! Wake up! Your enemy the devil, like a roaring lion, prowls around looking for someone to devour. Stand up to him, firm in your faith.' The passage goes on to remind us that our fellow Christians in this world are going through the same kinds of suffering (1 Peter 5.8-9). The devil and his entourage, the demonic spirits, would appear to be figments of imagination and mere superstition to contemporary thought inasmuch as unusual phenomena can more plausibly be explained by natural causes, so much so that it is always right to seek a rational explanation for any unusual occurrence even if remotely feasible. But there are occasions when there is such a concatenation of bizarre phenomena that the person or the premises attacked appear to be under the influence of evil spirits far beyond the explanation of anything in the vicinity. It is easy enough to shrug off the matter with amused indifference if one is not personally involved, but those closer at hand cannot afford to assume such comfortable detachment. Finally they will be advised to seek the help of an exorcist, or minister of deliverance; the two essential requirements for such a person are keen psychic and personal sensitivity and the authority to expel noxious influences. These influences should be sent to God's caring love and not just out of sight or, worse still, to the outer darkness where there will be weeping and grinding of teeth, a metaphor for eternal damnation especially favoured by Matthew (see 8.12; 13.42, 50; 22.13; 24.51; 25.30).

In fact, all created things, pleasant and unpleasant alike, are subject to the divine creative will. In the words of the Nicene Creed, 'I believe in one God, the Father Almighty, creator of heaven and earth, and of all things visible and invisible' (or 'of all that is, seen and unseen' in the contemporary liturgy). It follows that the darkness of creation is as much God's work as what we describe as the light. The truth is that much so-called light is judged as such by the immediately comforting effects it has on human contentment; the later spiritual influences may be distinctly less impressive.

Thinking along these lines, it often strikes one how even ferocious animals and poisonous snakes have an important role to play in modifying our ecological environment. This they do by destroying such living creatures as feed on their environment without any restraint, and left to their own devices would rapidly procreate without any restraint until the world was overcrowded and widespread famine the inevitable outcome. Humans, with their vastly superior mental equipment, can restrain their procreative activity in accordance with their intelligence and religious allegiance. Such intellectual checks and balances are not to be found amongst our humbler animal brethren, and they therefore are liable to starve in times of famine. Of course, humans can also suffer likewise during periods of widespread famine; a good biblical example is described in 2 Kings 6.24–7.20. The case contrasts sharply with King Solomon's famous judgement where two mothers fought over a dead infant who had probably been overlain by one of them, one mother then subtly removing the living baby from the other while she was asleep. The mother noticed that the dead child in her arms was not hers, and created a commotion about the trick played upon her, and brought the case to the king for a final judgement. He ordered his sword to be brought so that he could cut the child in half. The responsible person remained unmoved by this threat to the infant's life, whereas the real mother was so horrified that she was prepared rather to let her baby go to the other woman than see the child die (1 Kings 3.16-28). Love is indeed the test of truth: 'Many waters cannot quench love, neither can the floods drown it: if a man would give all the substance of his house for love, it would utterly be contemned' (Song of Songs 8.7), a beautiful quotation from the Authorized Version of the Bible.

Why are some creatures unpleasant, even dangerous, to the majority of their fellow beings? Obviously no one can answer such a question without a thoroughly egoistical bias, yet the struggle for life is the way to mastery, whether the victor is a plant, an animal or a human. We know nothing about the 'inner life' of a plant, and only mere glimpses illuminate our imagination about the psychic life of an animal. Some animals, those well domesticated in fact; can apparently make good relationships with humans; the most poignant evidence is the obvious grief many show when their owners die or move away to new homes. The fidelity of guide dogs towards their blind charges is another stirring example. There is no doubt that love brings out the best in all of us, whereas hatred evokes a correspondingly negative response. Remember that hatred may manifest itself as derision, cruelty, injustice or prejudice involving race, sex and lifestyle – to name only a few destructive impulses and hostile responses. When we consider how we respond to an unfriendly approach from a stranger, we are soon aware of an unpleasant emanation proceeding from them. The person is likely to exhibit one or more of the qualities I have already mentioned, and the hatred has a most unpleasant psychic effect that shows itself in the form of severe emotional depletion, which is a type of depression. The offensive person is clearly being 'used', and is sometimes called a 'channel', for powerful psychic energies coming through them but not originating from them. They are obviously ill-disposed to the victim, but do not know exactly what they are doing. This state of affairs is distinctly different from that of someone who bears a long-standing grudge or even inveterate hatred against another person; here too there are malign psychic energies being emitted, but they are personal in origin rather than demonic.

So what then is the nature of these demonic agencies, seen metaphorically as our adversary, the devil? I personally feel that what we call 'evil' is part of the divine creation, almost the divine will, for without the constant challenge to grow in spiritual awareness and stature, by which I mean becoming less self-centred and more dedicated to the welfare of all our fellow creatures (the vegetable and animal groups as well as the human one), the more we would remain stuck in an all too easy complacency. This is the type of heaven conjured up by some religious and spiritualistic groups, as was indicted in the last chapter. I do not simply accept a permissive view of evil – that it is an inevitable part of human nature which we have to accept as best we can – on the contrary, I see that it plays a paradoxical part in the divine economy.

Consider, for instance, Jesus' teaching in Luke 13.1–5, on the surface cold and very disheartening.

> At that time some people came and told him about the Galileans whose blood Pilate had mixed with their sacrifices. He answered them: 'Do you suppose that, because these Galileans suffered this fate, they must have been greater sinners than anyone else in Galilee? No, I tell you; but unless you repent, you will all of you come to the same end. Or the eighteen people who were killed when the tower fell on them at Siloam – do you imagine they must have been more guilty than all the other people living in Jerusalem? No, I tell you; but unless you repent, you will all come to an end like theirs.'

In other words, God visits calamity on his creatures, especially the human with its high intelligence, in order to train them for higher things. If we sincerely repent, we shall no longer be waylaid by a particular vice or bad habit, but instead we will almost inevitably move from the domination of the self-centred ego consciousness that looks for satisfaction above all else to a genuine concern for the welfare of other creatures. The final product of this more profound concern is a warmth of affection that may culminate in love, initially between two people but eventually among many more. Material success tends to separate people as they guard their own personal interests, while a natural or national disaster brings all members of the group close together.

It may be objected that this point of view, though doubtless philosophical, is wretched in terms of the very love I have been expounding, and I would not dispute this, but I do remember that our lives on this planet are a mere parenthesis in eternity. 'Do not store up for yourselves treasure on earth, where moth and rust destroy, and thieves break in and steal, but store up treasure in heaven, where neither moth nor rust will destroy, nor thieves break in and steal. For where your treasure is, there will your heart be also' (Matthew 6.19-21). The demonic spirits are here to test and train us, though few of us are sufficiently spiritually astute to understand what the battle for our lives on earth really entails. 'Now is the hour of judgement for this world; now shall the prince of this world be driven out. And when I am lifted up from the earth I shall draw everyone to myself' (John 12.31-2). The 'prince of this world' is the devil and his army, and their work consists largely in terrifying uncommitted people by inexplicable psychic phenomena so that they are easily seduced into any mode of behaviour that promises rapid relief.

When an atmosphere is demonically infested, the normal thought processes of the obsessed person are radically impaired. Frank demonic possession is extremely rare and is associated with typical signs that we shall later consider. Much more typical is an atmosphere of gloom and foreboding that paralyses the mental and emotional faculties of all but the most stalwart person in the locality. Often the malign influence appears to emanate from a particular individual, and those with a gift of clairvoyance may see a zone, or aura, around them, without having any prior information, yet knowing that they are dealing with a source of evil. The essence of evil is the desire to seduce another person and then to feed parasitically on them. In the end the victim is discarded barely alive or even dead while the predator enjoys their fill. These predatory people seem to possess a 'psychic constitution' that especially lays them open to demonic infestation. Furthermore, their way of life brings them into especially close contact with the demonic powers that pervade the universe.

People who boast about their piety and generally faultless lifestyle may be at least as vulnerable to demonic attack, or even demonic infestation, as the more sinful among us who do not make any show of their moral excellence. Good examples of this danger of spiritual pride – which in fact can never be other than an illusion about our deep-rooted sinfulness that is conveniently though only temporarily occluded by a mist of complacent self-reliance – are to be found repeatedly in the Old Testament, especially in the prophetic books of Amos and Jeremiah. But it is in the teaching of Jesus that the truth is explicitly spelt out, as in the parable of the Pharisee and the tax-collector (Luke 18.9–14) or in Jesus' severe criticism of those people who exhibit their piety in the fulsome performance of the religious duties of their faith, especially fasting (Matthew 6.2–18). They may evoke the admiration of their peers for a short period of time, but all this show is soon forgotten by the fickle human mind. There is a lasting and completely trustworthy concern for us in our Creator alone; in the Divine Presence we can assimilate the undemanding love which would never allow us to be sacrificed for a selfish ideal, but instead leaves us to grow into the full stature of mature humans.

Therefore the most certain way of assessing an unclean psychic atmosphere is by noting the effect it produces on our temperament, our present mood, and our intolerance to various kinds of people, varying from strangers to our close associates. If an unaccountable hostility towards someone we believe we know quite well suddenly assails us, it could be that we are the victim of an attack by a demonic spirit which has found a very pleasant home in a vulnerable mind.

> When an unclean spirit comes out of someone it wanders over the desert sands seeking a resting-place; and if it finds none, it says, 'I will go back to the home I left.' So it returns and finds the house swept clean and tidy. It goes off and collects seven other spirits more wicked than itself, and they all come in and settle there; and in the end that person's plight is worse than before. (Luke 11.24-6)

We can learn much from this well-known parable. First of all, a so-called healing – whether physical, mental or psychical – is never to be taken for granted. It is always a special gift from God, and if it is squandered or even disregarded by not allowing it to effect a change in our lifestyle, not only will its fruits be lost but the promising benefit will be followed a little while later by a prolonged period of lamentation when we compare our present distress with the only recently past time of relief. The recurrent periods of suffering recounted in the Old Testament illustrate this sequence most poignantly.

Jesus performs the glorious work of salvation for all the creation, especially his fellow humans. The end of his work in the world is his betrayal and murder mounted by the collective forces of darkness, also called the demonic powers or demonic spirits. In his case there is, I believe, good reason to believe in an actual personal resurrection on the third day after his death, because a number of people who had known him very well while he was still alive in the flesh saw him closely and even heard him speak to them. To me, the various post-resurrection appearances come into the category of clairvoyance and clairaudience. I do not accept solid materializations such as some spiritualists claim, nor do I believe that Jesus' physical body continued to survive in an earthly form. It was, on the contrary, in the psychic realm where it may still be actively at work, refreshing and rendering increasingly holy a very intermediate state of existence where the souls of those in the purgatorial state are being progressively cleansed and educated for the work in front of them. To me, the most convincing proof of Jesus' resurrection was the emotional resurrection of the disciples; who were previously broken with shame and disappointment, and terrified by the fear of sharing their Master's fate. Some life-shattering event must have taken place to have provoked this change of heart and mind, a so-called 'metanoia'. The subsequent worldwide spread of Christianity would appear to substantiate this probability, especially when we remember the early persecutions continuing well into the fourth century.

The psychic means of communication, whether friendly or demonic, are described as telepathic. Telepathy may be defined as the communication from one mind to another at a distance other than through the known senses. Parapsychology, traditionally known as psychical research, is as we have already noted in chapters 1 and 2 infuriatingly unpredictable; its phenomena appear out of the blue. For instance, a sequence of telepathic messages may arrest the attention of two friends or colleagues, and then for no apparently good reason the sequence shuts down. Emotional rapport is a necessary factor in telepathic communication, but most people have only very poorly developed psychic faculties. The intellectually accomplished type of person, who has great difficulty in accepting the very existence of the paranormal dimension of communication, will know little indeed of the subject because of prior prejudice against anything other than materialistic explanations for all phenomena. Such a person is at a considerable disadvantage in self-knowledge and in accepting the spiritual component of reality. By this I mean the supreme reality that religious people call God, remembering that there is an important distinction between religion and spirituality. Spirituality is the spontaneous recognition of the soul as it responds to the divine grace, whereas religion is a set of rules, doctrines, dogmas and general ways of life that should lead us on the spiritual path whose end is the knowledge of God.

It might nevertheless be argued that psychic insensitivity is a safe option; even if it deadens a person's response to some amazing experiences, even the direct apprehension of God so far as this is available to human consciousness. Certainly psychic sensitivity opens us up to the world of demonic spirits in no uncertain way, but then this is an aspect of our life's experience, comparable in its typically occult way to such mundane misfortunes as being swindled by criminals, falling in with doubtful characters in our worldly life, or being subject to physical misfortunes such as terrorist attacks or more ordinary civilian or military injuries. I am not suggesting that any of these is necessarily a manifestation of demonic activity, though I do believe that God is in charge of his universe and capable of bringing light to instances of individual darkness when there is repentance together with the courage to proceed onward. We also require the faith to trust in the generosity of life provided we are sensible enough to use it wisely, not only for ourselves but for the family also. 'Family' starts on a very personal level but must proceed to include all living animals if it is to be real in its entirety. The demonic aspect of reality shows itself in a personal destructiveness whose aim is complete dominance of the creation; it prefers to use and enslave the human victim rather than killing it outright. The reason for this is that the demonic spirit tends to feed parasitically on its victim, killing it only when it has completed its primarily destructive work. Therefore once again one must avoid colluding in ignorance with demonic spirits, a collusion that commences as an innocent enough dabbling with the occult.

But returning to the point just made; is a psychically insensitive individual more to be envied for his or her relative immunity to psychic attack from afar? In fact such a person is more rather than less vulnerable inasmuch as a sensitive person will have acquired a degree of psychic defence over the years of experience behind them, whereas the psychically ignorant individual, when suddenly and unexpectedly assailed by a demonic spirit, is very liable to suffer severe psychological damage which shows itself in anxiety, insomnia and a tendency to distrust the motives of other people, even those whom were previously well known and highly regarded. The sudden feeling of insecurity also manifests itself in guarding property and money very obsessively. Those with psychological knowledge would have little difficulty in identifying the state I have described as a paranoid reaction, and since few psychiatrists have any knowledge of, or sympathy towards, psychic matters, the condition may remain unrelieved for some time.

The right procedure in such a case is for a minister of deliverance to expel (or exorcize) the demonic spirit from its present abode, but making sure that it has a good home (a place of loving concern) to which to proceed. The matter has already been considered in relation to demonic spirits who return to their previous abode accompanied by more of their kind because they were not moved on elsewhere, which in effect means into the care of God. It is a basic principle that every created object has its place in the scheme of things. Noxious agents, when they have necessarily been annihilated by humans, continue to live on in the divine consciousness similarly to the 'useful' orders, for God loves all created things. If this were not the case none of us would survive for even the briefest moment. Every living form, however useless or noxious it may appear to us, has its use in the divine economy. In the instance of disease-producing organisms, not only do they cut down the number of rapidly reproducing living forms but, by their destructive effect, enable those animals who survive (including humans) to grow in strength and complexity. Where there is no challenge there is little growth, for most of us prefer the status quo where we can happily drop off to sleep and depend on someone else for our sustenance. When that 'someone else' is God himself, we can lose all sense of personal responsibility such as is the situation of our animal brethren. This explains the special privilege of being a human as well as the pain and suffering associated with that privilege. The essence of that pain and suffering is our exquisite psychic sensitivity. The pain that sensitivity bequeaths on us follows on our mutual membership of the body of humanity, as we noted in chapter 1.

In the hierarchy of relationships between humans and the rest of the world it is no surprise that the most intimate connection is a psychic one, for it joins at the level of the soul. From this soul contact flow emotions both positive and negative as well as thoughts of various intensities. The body is our amazingly sensitive instrument for working in a world of ever-evolving ideas, discoveries and enterprises, which in turn are centred around the love and will of God. It is of note that God's will is freedom for his most brilliant creature, the human, and those who believe that subservience to God is the human absolute duty are far from the mark. Thus Jesus says in John 8.32, 'You will know the truth, and the truth will set you free.' This freedom is a rupture from the past sinful attitudes and actions, as the passage goes on to explain to the Jews who are indignant that anyone should suggest that they have ever been slaves to any temporal power. But Jesus is speaking about slavery to sin in its manifold forms.

The knowledge of God comes from an enlightened

conscience which is illuminated from the Divine Source itself. The light clears the psychic sense, which is comparable in its own right to the eye or the ear and those parts of the brain that receive visual and auditory impressions from these peripheral organs of sensation. Then we *know* intuitively with a confidence that moves beyond personal judgement with its inevitable traces of prejudice, no matter how far we go to eliminate these from our mind. In fact, this enlightened communication, which is also direct communion, with God is an experience of pure joy; because, as when we receive the elements of the Eucharist, we are given the supreme privilege as an act of pure grace. We do not earn it, nor can we do anything to receive it except by living as charitably and lovingly as possible. This mode of living is furthermore a part of our everyday life and not something assumed for a definite purpose. As we continue along this path of grace, so our psychic faculties are cleansed and we can begin to see more clearly that which is absolutely invisible to most of our peers.

It would appear that we have two basic means of acquiring information about our local and mundane situation. The first and most obvious is our native intelligence which processes the data provided by our sense organs and integrates them into a system of thoughts and ideas. It is this cognitive means of communication that brings our various experiences into a system of communication whereby we can compare different perceptions and conceptions rationally with other people. This 'knowing' faculty is the basis of teaching and learning, and its end is the education of a group of people to achieve the work necessary for their survival. This way of communication is a feature of the civilized human mind; therefore being most well developed in humans who have lived in relatively recent eras. By contrast, even the ape family have only a rudimentary intelligence in comparison with their human relatives.

The other mode of getting knowledge about our situation, whether local or mundane, is one that transcends the native intelligence completely. This is the psychic way of knowledge, and is at least as powerful in intellectually indifferent people as in the learned. There is incidentally a subtle difference between the intellect and intelligence. The first has the capacity to grasp truth with an intuitive certainty even though the person themself may be poorly educated. The second is the capacity to learn rapidly by experience; as such it is invaluable in teaching and learning, and is the basis of education. Intelligence requires no recommendation, but the intellect is cultivated by the person's way of life which separates them from the trivia of much everyday activity. It is sad that so much of the intellect has been clouded by a dominant, scientific approach to reality, an approach that is oblivious of any model of truth except the crassly materialistic. And yet, to be fair, this approach is both measurable and repeatable whereas the indefinite psychic intimations of reality can neither be produced at will nor measured. The entire study of paranormal phenomena is frustrating. It is a good general rule that the type of person who boasts of their psychic capacities is seldom accurate in their assessment of those capacities, and often they are unpleasantly egotistical. The true psychic has a spiritual aura around them; humility, not exhibitionism, is the mark of their gift, which in their hands is a true one.

6

Psychic Incursions of Property

———————

Unaccountable phenomena occurring in localities sufficient to render them virtually uninhabitable are a recurrent theme in the world's history. In the Old Testament, God comes to the aid of his erring children, often when they have just reached the point of destruction either by natural disasters or the victory of their enemies. God produces his way of relief by the use of malign psychic phenomena aimed at the enemy, who, though vastly superior in material numbers to the Israelites, are frightened into abandoning their position and possessions and fleeing away to the safety of their own abode, which may be thousands of miles from the present place of conflict.

One of the most dramatic instances is recorded in 2 Kings 6—7 in respect of the relief of a population on the verge of starvation during the course of a very severe famine. This famine has already been alluded to in chapter 5.

The king of Israel, one of the Bible's numerous typically evil characters, had subsequently come to destroy Elisha, since he believed that God had clearly planned all the misery, and Elisha was God's prophet. Elisha, however, made the astonishing prophecy that within a day such common articles of food as flour and barley would sell at a very cheap rate. On a purely rational level this seemed quite impossible even if the drought, which was the cause of the famine, was broken instantaneously by a gigantic spell of rain, for a considerable time would need to elapse before the vegetation would start to grow once more. Nevertheless, Elisha's prophecy came to pass, for the next day four men who were afflicted by a relatively common skin disease (traditionally called leprosy, though this diagnosis does not tally with the modern definition of the disease) were dallying at the entrance of the city gate. They were debating their grim future, and decided that staying in the confines of Samaria, which was besieged by the Assyrian army commanded by King Ben-Hadad (2 Kings 6.24), presented no worse fate than their present situation. And so at dusk the four of them set out for the camp, but when they reached its confines there was not a soul to be found. What apparently had happened was that the soldiers were confronted by the clamour of chariots and horses which resembled a great army, which the Aramaeans believed came from the Hittites and Egyptians, whom the king of Israel had hired to attack them.

And so in the dusk they fled, abandoning their tents, animals and various possessions, including silver, gold and clothing. At first the dazed men kept the news and the material wealth to themselves, but soon a warmer conscience rose up in them, and they spread the good news to the royal palace of the king of Israel. At first he could not accept the veracity of this apparent retreat of the Aramaean forces, believing that they were merely acting to entice the Israelites to enter the camp, after which they would reappear and destroy the Israelites completely. In passing, it is noteworthy that at an earlier period the Israelites performed a similar stratagem against the inhabitants of Ai (Joshua 8.1–25). The racial memory no doubt persisted, especially as the destruction was preceded by a terrible reverse, when an Israelite force was radically repulsed before the later spectacular victory; the cause of this earlier defeat was the avarice of an Israelite who coveted something from Ai that had fallen on God's curse (Joshua 7). In the present instance the officers to whom the king confided his doubts suggested that they form a team with the few surviving horses still available, in order to confirm the men's story. They found matters substantially as had been reported and the whole way from the camp to the Jordan strewn with clothes and gear which the panic-stricken Aramaeans had thrown away. Thus Elisha's prophecy was fulfilled when the starving Israelites were able to partake freely of the Aramaeans' provisions long before any change in the weather had occurred.

A far more dramatic and terrible fate was in store for the Assyrian army some hundred and fifty years later. Under their brutal and very powerful King Sennacherib they had threatened the complete destruction of Israel under its beneficent King Hezekiah, and their boastfulness had become intolerable. Isaiah made a strong prophecy that the king of Assyria would not enter Jerusalem, let alone attack it. On the contrary he would return by the same way as he came, for God was determined to save the city for the sake of his servant David. That very night the angel of God struck down 185,000 men in the Assyrian camp. In the morning when it was time to arise, there they lay, so many corpses. Sennacherib did indeed strike camp and returned home, staying in Nineveh where his two sons murdered him and escaped into the territory of Ararat (2 Kings 19.35-7).

In the first narrative, God intervenes to save his people by terrifying their enemies but not actually destroying them. In the second narrative, the rescue of Israel is accomplished by a wholesale destruction of the enemy forces, but the nature of the destroying force is obscure. God is, of course, the source of all things good and bad alike, as we considered in chapter 1, but we are entitled to eliminate deleterious elements in our environment. This includes hostile living forms also, which I believe have been created to accelerate the development of the higher forms of life. Development proceeds by the mechanism of challenge, and this entails not only much strife but also the ultimate destruction of the challenging agent, unless by the grace of God that agent evolves into something primarily useful and ultimately noble. As any agnostic would add, the more highly a species evolves, the more terribly its destructive powers might manifest themselves; in highly civilized humans creativity attaining nearly divine proportions has been accompanied with the most serious defects of character sufficient to lead to wholesale persecutions and bloodshed.

This apparent diversion from the theme of psychic incursions of property finds its justification in the fact that usually the powerful agent producing these hostile invasions is the human living in the property, whether at the present time or at a previous period. One example is the poltergeist that was considered in chapter 2, but this is a nuisance rather than a very harmful presence. Sometimes properties may be haunted by extremely terrifying atmospheres that may produce such depression that nobody who is psychically sensitive could bear to be within reach of them. The human that may be found living in the precincts of the locality has an unpleasant feeling to them: they cannot look one straight in the face but often exude a suspicious charm, though their manner of speech is tortuous and its content a maze of insinuations. In short, one is intuitively uncomfortable with the person, and is relieved to retire from their company as soon as possible. The criminal classes of society show many of these characteristics, and an experienced policeman will identify them quite easily. But many such people do not involve themselves in petty crime, but in much more dangerous activities that aim at undermining individuals, families or society itself. The paradoxical feature of all this malign description is that the person concerned is blissfully unaware of the danger in which they live and the potential harm they may cause, if indeed they are not already causing.

If one is actually sensitive psychically, one can often discern a shadowy darkness around these people and also an unpleasant smell in their vicinity. This is quite distinct from the smell of a dirty person, which we all know from our own experience. This smell has an acutely pungent characteristic which reminds us of an unpleasant circumstance in the past, making the heart palpitate and the mind quicken with anxiety. It is recognized that the sense of smell, though the most primitive of the five senses in the human, who relies primarily on sight, hearing and touch, is imbued with a strong psychic element. It makes us aware or else reminds us of past happenings that in their turn produce strong emotional effects. It is in this way that the psychic sense plays its part in modifying our attitudes and behaviour; at its best filling us with hope but at its worst depressing us with unpleasant forebodings. It is noteworthy in passing that the senses of smell and taste, though quite separate, work together when we eat a meal: the four tastes of sweet, sour, salt and bitter are modified by the faculty of smell which plays a vital part in the savour of a meal. When the faculty of smell is temporarily obliterated as during a severe nasal cold, we can taste our food as well as ever, but it lacks its essential flavour by which we recognize it for what it is. When a piece of food reminds us of a long past event and evokes a psychic sensitivity, it is the smell associated with it that evokes the emotional reaction. On the whole, at least in my experience, the psychic responses to food are more often unpleasant than pleasant, a sad proof that 'the prince of the world' is still far from conquered in the souls of many of God's creatures, for we are all parts of the one body, to quote St Paul once more.

Rather more frequently, however, I believe that the human agent who has caused the trouble is an unquiet spirit of the dead, such as we have considered in chapter 3. Their soul is not at rest, and it will continue to produce unpleasant repercussions until its presence is properly acknowledged. Only then will it be in a position to move onwards to the light of God's love and away from the present all-encompassing darkness. The type of person who is especially liable to remain earthbound after their physical death is the one whose life on earth was dominated by entirely selfish pursuits. Since their awareness was almost completely limited to their concerns, they may fail to recognize the extreme change that has overtaken them, and proceed along a well-worn course which they take to be their usual life on earth. They become very indignant when they discover that their home is now occupied by a stranger who, in their eyes, has no right to be there. All this incidentally reminds us of the temporary nature of human possessions; they are here today and gone from us tomorrow. Our stewardship is of short duration even at its best, for we are soon put to bed in the far country of death even at the zenith of our activities. Our achievement is measured primarily by the effect we have had on the lives of those around us, whether they have been hurt by our influence or healed of their infirmities both physical and spiritual. We are most helpful when we forget ourselves in serving other people; on the other hand, when we place ourselves at the head of activities, we cause only disturbances in the psychic atmosphere. If this is true even while we are alive on earth and our psychic sensitivity is at least a little under the control of a dense physical body, when we die we can cause much greater havoc on earth at least among those who are especially vulnerable. It is this type of entity that causes the most powerful effect on the local environment, and its connection with it when it inhabited a physical body explains its continued attachment to it later.

If a terrible crime has been committed in the area – especially if justice has not been properly carried out – the disturbance will be potentially very unpleasant. The entity is inflamed by a combination of fear and anger for the injustice it feels has been committed against it. If a person believes that they have been especially wrongfully treated, they may be inspired to curse the individual whom they blame or else the locality in which the wrongful action had taken place. We will consider the matter of curses in a subsequent chapter, but suffice to add at this stage that the power of a malediction is far from being illusory, and can cause serious trouble. Hatred emits a nasty odour like the one already described, and this smell is merely an outer, and at least slightly apprehensible, sign of something going seriously amiss in the emotional life of an individual or the community at large.

Therefore psychic incursions of a malign type affecting property can arise from both contaminated humans and their demonic sources. The value of all the trouble they cause is that they awaken the human agent at least – we cannot identify anyone on any other level – from the slumber of complacency, so that they are impelled to progress onwards to psychical mastery, which they discover cannot be achieved without a prior spiritual battle of high intensity among those who are in the thick of spiritual conflict for which there appears to be no logical reason let alone a solution. 'And, as we know, all things work together for good for those who love God' (Romans 8.28). The way of approaching apparently insuperable evil is by confronting it in love. This love is Christ in us, the hope of a glory to come (Colossians 1.27). This does not automatically mean that we should turn the other cheek, thereby actually avoiding an embarrassing if not far more lethal encounter with a particularly unpleasant person, or for that matter any other living creature. There is a time for conflict and a time for reconciliation just as there is a time for victory and a time for defeat. This last is the most certain of all at least in terms of earthly existence, but the closer we attain to the stature of Jesus, the less relevant do the very concepts of defeat and victory become on an immediately mundane level of existence, for by the experience of our own particular tragic failure, symbolized as the cross in Christian terms, we come to know ourselves as eternal beings – and our various enemies that seemed such enormous eternal beings also.

All this sounds theoretical as well as ludicrously comforting in terms of reason, or common sense, and so it is too.

But life is more than reason, essential as this undoubtedly is for daily living. Repeating a thought from 1 Corinthians 15.32, 'If the dead are never raised to life, "Let us eat and drink, for tomorrow we die."' If living is nothing more than the sustenance of the body, St Paul's ironic dictum fits perfectly, but if we have an expanded view of life – one that transcends the physical body – we are all vulnerable to psychic assault. If we are wise we lead chaste, orderly lives so that our inner resources are strengthened for the inevitable conflict ahead of us as part of our life's history. The means of this strengthening are first and last prayer, which alone brings us into the Divine Presence where we are prepared for an ordeal that has no end on this side of the grave.

Prayer, in my opinion, is not to be seen so much as a way of protection against the dark forces that seem so often to dominate the world, as a means of our strengthening for the inevitable conflict. The difference between protection and strengthening is quite subtle; the first separates us from evil, whereas the second offers no such guarding function, but gives us the resource to grow into full adulthood. In this state of enhanced spirituality we can serve God's purpose more profoundly by separating evil spirits from creation, at the same time weaning them from destructive tendencies and bringing them closer to God. St Paul puts this thought memorably in Ephesians 3.17–19, 'With deep roots and firm foundations may you, in company with all God's people, be strong to grasp what is the breadth and length and height and depth of Christ's love, and to know it, though it is beyond knowledge. So may you be filled with the very fullness of God.' This type of knowing is far beyond all rational understanding, for it reaches the mystical height of reality that cannot be defined except in negative terms.

The nearest positive concept of God is to be found in 1 John 4.16, 'God is love; he who dwells in love is dwelling in God, and God in him.' St Paul in 1 Corinthians 13 defines love in terms of the annulment of the dominating ego consciousness. Thus even giving away all our possessions and being prepared to sacrifice our very life does not bring us to love or to the knowledge of God (verse 3). Love, on the contrary, is known by its life-enhancing qualities: patience; kindness; an absence of conceit, boastfulness, rudeness and selfishness; and an unwillingness to take offence. Love keeps no score of wrongs, takes no pleasure in the sins of others. There is nothing it cannot face; there is no limit to its faith, its hope and its endurance. The most important quality comes right at the end of this recital: love will never come to an end (verses 4–8). It should be said that giving away all our possessions and being prepared to sacrifice our life itself in the cause of martyrdom for what we clearly see as the right action is strongly to be praised. But this mode of living should be a result of the qualities enumerated in 1 Corinthians 13.4–8; in other words, the way of decency should be an inevitable sequel of the life of love, and it should be essentially innocent of all conceit.

In this respect there are two types of innocence. The first affects us all indiscriminately when we are small children and gradually find our way in an increasingly complex world which is governed in the first place by our parents and teachers. The second type of innocence is to remain unsullied, though not untouched, by the temptations of the world when we have grown up into adult life. The world, the flesh and the devil are often presented as our essential agents of temptation. In the scheme of growth into something of the measure of the fullness of Christ that I accept – so that suffering, a fall into moral temptation, and cruel death are all part of a greater whole – I find St Paul's words in Ephesians 4.13 of great inspiration as well as comfort: 'Until we all attain to the unity inherent in our faith and in our knowledge of the Son of God – to mature manhood, measured by nothing less than the full stature of Christ'. Therefore in the second, or adult, type of innocence we remain inwardly pure even if we fail from time to time to attain the highest spirituality. The lives of the saints, and especially that notorious persecutor of the earliest Christians – St Paul – show that what matters most in adult life is not a childlike innocence of the world's ways, but a sincere urge to repentance that shows itself in a changed way of life, the way indeed of charity in the sense of a love to all our fellow creatures.

There can be little doubt that the adult type of innocence is of much greater use to society than the infantile one. Only the reformed sinner, once having had the courage and honesty to face the past without flinching, can really understand the psychology of their erring brethren. By contrast, the spontaneously 'good' person, who has had little experience of the world's greater problems, may easily remain judgemental; as may also those who have been emotionally 'converted' to an apparently impeccable faith which to them contains the whole truth, all other approaches being part of the temptations of the world, the flesh or the devil. We come to the interesting conclusion that the zenith of experience is innocence, a higher innocence that has grasped the inadequacy of worldly things in their own right. Such an innocence has tasted the fruits of personal sin and the relief of divine forgiveness. Thus the person is truly converted to the light of universal love.

And so we come once more to the Pauline dictum that all things work together for good to those who love God. The more we are in Christ, the more we are in the world also, but the world is no longer a wicked place; just as the present wicked age is now no longer as evil as before the advent of Christ (Galatians 1.4). The liberation effected by God in Christ has lifted the complete darkness of the world to the light of God's love as an earnest of good things to come.

The essential component of dealing with psychic incursions of property therefore is a cleansing and strengthening of the character of those living or working there. Once we grasp the essential fact of life that there is no power, even if we call it God himself, that will come in from outside to rake our chestnuts out of the fire, we can begin to assume a degree of personal responsibility. As we work with adult commitment to serve the world with all our inner resources, so we come closer to the real God, who is no longer a power from beyond us so much as a presence within us bringing us ever closer to the light. When we know this spiritual truth, which to interpolate Ephesians 3.19 once again, is in fact beyond knowledge, we can understand the famous aphorism of 1 John 4.18, 'In love there is no room for fear; indeed perfect love banishes fear.' No one can locate God, but his presence is necessarily known to us in terms of indwelling or immanence.

The transcendent God is dismissed quite glibly by non-believers as a manifestation of the material universe and its scientific mechanism, all of which is true in its own right. But how did it start, and where did its building blocks originate? In other words, the workings of the universe can be increasingly satisfactorily explained rationally, but its origin remains a mystery, for reason itself tells us that nothing cannot be the origin of anything. An infinite regression – a return to an earlier stage of development continued as far as the mind will penetrate or scientific research reveal – does not solve this problem. Only a non-material principle can begin to fathom and approach the mystery, inasmuch as this type of being, which could conveniently be identified with the supreme Creator, might be the source of all the material substance of the universe.

Clearly God is both transcendent and immanent. The scientist who is a believer will tend to recognize the Creator God who is transcendent of all his creation, while the mystic, who knows God as a deep personal presence in the soul, will from earliest youth know the immanent God whom St Paul identifies with 'Christ in you, the hope of glory' (Colossians 1.27). Both approaches are essential to a proper knowledge of the Divine, for together they illuminate different aspects of reality. These are the material and the spiritual. Both are equally important not only for our own survival but for the growth and development of the world. The basis of all truth is balance, something almost outside the scope of most humans. Those who opt for a material way end up in bodily death, while those who stress their allegiance to the spiritual path to the exclusion of worldly matters share exactly the same fate. Only those who give of themselves to both worldly and spiritual matters will contribute to the transformation of the world by a spirituality that finds its apogee in the resurrection body of Christ.

When we consider psychic incursions of property we see how non-material energy can impinge on material substance and cause damaging effects of varying degree. These may vary from the production of depressing or terrifying atmospheres to very clearly physical phenomena like an interference of the electricity supply or the water system. I have known incidents where wastepaper baskets have been mischievously overturned so that their contents have stained the surrounding carpet or else spoilt the atmosphere of the room in which they were located. Some of these episodes were clearly of the poltergeist type, but others have been more malicious. It is the atmosphere pervading the affected locality that defines the nature of the psychic emanation and suggests its source.

I personally have never known an instance of total, permanent disappearance of any object that could be attributed to a psychic disturbance, but in the shorter term I have on more than one occasion been driven nearly frantic by the apparent loss of an article, which I have quite deliberately placed in a certain site, only to find it nearby – days, weeks or even months later. On some occasions when I had steeled myself to the loss of the article, it suddenly turned up near the place where I had remembered leaving it. All this could, of course, be attributed to a faulty memory, but the deliberate placing of the object makes this an inadequate explanation as far as I am concerned. And why should it return to its previous site after a long period of disappearance confirmed by repeated checking? In my own experience there are some places in various houses which I have visited where this strange phenomenon is liable to occur. Whether this unusual occurrence is set in motion by my own psychic capacity, or whether it is known to others in the household also I do not know, because too much investigation along these lines could appear quite impolite, even invidious to one's relationship with the owners of the house, unless they by chance or fell necessity broached the subject. This sort of conversation can also bring to light the experience of a ghost that various people are witnessing, though seldom all in even one small household, so variable are individual psychic capacities likely to be.

As I mentioned in chapter 2, ghosts are non-material deposits of obsessional material that have arisen from past experiences of people who have dwelt in a particular place. They are insubstantial, but frequently bear an invidious emotional charge apart from their actual presence, which can hardly fail to produce some feeling of discomfort ranging from sharing a space with a foreign entity to sheer terror following a psychic invasion. Of course, some ghosts are almost part of the household furniture of a dwelling place, and may even be great favourites, especially among the young. The thought of exorcizing them could be quite shocking to this type of person, but they would clearly come into the category of the lovable eccentrics on whose witness the world depends. The form of a ghost may closely resemble the appearance of the person when they were living in the locality, perhaps centuries ago. Sometimes a ghost may be a 'thought form', the imagined or imprinted appearance of a person who lived in the place at a previous period.

One case with which I was involved concerned the recurrent appearance of a nun running down a flight of stairs. It seemed that centuries ago a nun who had stolen a small amount of money was eventually found out. In order to escape she had run precipitately down the staircase, but during the course of her flight she had fallen and sustained fatal injuries. Apparently the horror of the incident had imprinted itself on her mind and perhaps the community's mind also. It had persisted as a permanent psychic landmark which seemed to reveal itself in the presence of some psychically sensitive people. Some of these saw the form of a young woman on the stairs, others a nun fully dressed in a habit, and others still were aware of someone falling on the stairs accompanied by screaming. I believe that, for a time after our death, each of us becomes a discarnate entity, before we move on to higher things according to the worthiness of our life on earth. But I do not believe such an entity was present in this case. The form was a psychic imprint of a horrifying episode, similar in its own way to a tape recording of a speech or a concert. Dabbling in this area can encourage the form to persist. It can live on for ever even though the incident ended in a matter of minutes, or at the very most hours.

Dealing with thought forms is quite simple. The principle is to sweep them away from our world just as we would some paper from the floor. Therefore one lifts up the thought form to God's care by strong prayer, asking that it may be dissolved according to God's will. It certainly need cause no one to fear. The concern is that it may take its rightful place in God's universe, and not remain sequestered in a backwater, speaking metaphorically. I should mention in passing that the young nun continued to appear as a thought form long after the convent where she had died had been closed. The precincts were now a fine charitable foundation with a somewhat secular ethos, though not hostile to Christianity. In the greater life beyond death, time and space take on such a different form that our worldly concepts cease to fit in a greater understanding of reality.

The unquiet dead can also appear as ghosts, but in this situation they show their independent personalities, making their emotional responses very obvious. In my experience the unquiet dead manifest themselves much more frequently by the emotional atmosphere they set up than by any visual phenomena, so much so that I tend to regard ghosts with interest rather than alarm.

The most important function of a minister of deliverance in dealing with a family which had come in contact with what appears to be a ghost is to reassure them of the probable nature of the situation but, of course, before any authoritative statement can be made to them, the minister themself needs to be psychic, so as to assess the situation accurately. It is as inadequate to minimize the significance of a ghost as to proceed with a dramatic exorcism without delay. As any physician knows, there is no universal panacea for any disease; each has its own treatment, if indeed the disease is as yet curable by any means that we know. Nevertheless, there is one weapon, available to all of us: rapt prayer.

As I have already explained, this may not always be immediately effective for the purpose that is concerning us, but it gives us strength for the trial awaiting us. Likewise the minister must be quite literally steeped in prayer if they are to do their work effectively. Prayer alone brings us into the Divine Presence, but we also need psychic sensitivity for deliverance work. The combination of the two is rare, and it is for this reason that effective exorcists will always be rare individuals. It is far easier to cast doubts on the integrity of anyone who is claimed to have psychic gifts (the person is always unwise to make such a claim themselves, remembering that self-praise is no recommendation), because the attitude of most people in sophisticated society is one of compulsive agnosticism to which more than a little pride is often added. On the other hand, ignorant people are often notoriously superstitious and fear-ridden, so that any unusual occurrence can easily assume a demonic or divine character. The ideal type of person is one who is well educated by always being open to new possibilities; who can see that the world, and even their own life, is not a fixed system, but capable of enormous expansion. Such a person combines within themselves humility and courage, both qualities being essential for an effective exorcist. The supreme paradox of our life on earth is that 'the prince of the world' is evil, and necessarily so, but even from this source of evil in its darkest intensity good *can* arise and fulfil itself in glory.

7

Demonic Attacks on People

This subject is one of the most controversial of all in the psychic field, as well as being fraught with great fear and illusion. Therefore it is very useful to confront the matter directly and see what it contains and how we may deal with it. The first principle to note is that demonic attacks are very unusual in healthy conditions, by which I mean among people whose lives are relatively wholesome. This does not mean that they should have attained sanctity, but simply that their way of life contains elements of the Ten Commandments and even a few precepts from the Sermon on the Mount. They will fall from grace repeatedly, but will acknowledge their backsliding to God, asking in deep prayer not only for forgiveness but also for the strength to resist the assaults of the evil one more successfully in the future. The strength makes us increasingly resistant to the assaults of the evil one, who can conveniently be called the angel of darkness, or the devil. It is when we fall away completely from the spiritual practice of prayer and especially from the presence of God that we are vulnerable to the attack of the forces of darkness.

Most people would not even entertain the possibility of a demonic assault, so antagonistic is this approach to current thinking. This is no great misfortune, for the whole subject of demonic attack moves dangerously into the fields of superstition, fanaticism and sheer terror, so that our normal thinking processes – which even at their most inadequate are vital for our worldly activities day by day – can be easily eclipsed. It is for this reason that the subject should be addressed with some degree of responsibility, remembering that God is the Creator and ultimate protector of all his creation. People who have strong psychic sensitivity are open to emotional and deeply personal facets of the personalities of other people that are hidden from the great majority of the population. It is this aspect of hiddenness that is termed 'the occult', and its deliberate investigation cannot be approved under any circumstances, because no matter what the practitioner may believe, such work is performed out of a curiosity that has its end in personal gain. And how easily we delude ourselves when we are fulfilling our own desires, especially when there is an attractive prize at the end which we may or may not share with others, but always remain in charge of operations! This is typically the temptation of the devil.

I should make it clear at once that this decidedly sweeping condemnation does not include genuinely scientific workers involved in parapsychological research. They should exhibit an integrity common to all research workers, and their aim, like that of all dedicated scientists, is the advancement of knowledge. In fact, parapsychological research has to date had a distinctly negative flavour, because psychical phenomena cannot be summoned to order and therefore compared experimentally. The nearest we can come to accepting the reality of psychical phenomena – to demonstrate that they are not merely coincidences occurring sporadically during a period of time – is to note that similar phenomena are reported continually in the lives of many different types of people. In other words, such proof as is available about the reality of the psychic dimension is not repeatable and therefore not reliable in scientific terms. What proof is available comes rather from the realm of personal experience and could be called phenomenological.

If, for instance, a group of people has repeated experiences of telepathy, precognition or clairvoyance (such as seeing a ghost), which they know to be accurately reported, there comes a time when the matter cannot be dismissed merely as meaningless coincidence. This is the usual explanation for all anomalous phenomena by agnostic observers, but it needs in some way to be put into a larger framework of reality, even if at present we are still groping for that framework. It would certainly appear that the psychic field transcends the boundaries of rationality, and it could well be that a different type of experimentation will need to be devised to establish its reality in a broader context and to test and measure its own capacity.

None of this disturbs me, for as William Wordsworth wrote in his sonnet, 'The River Dudden', no. 34 'Afterthought': 'And if, as toward the silent tomb we go, Through love, through hope, and faith's transcendent dower, We feel that we are greater than we know'. Words like these of sheer beauty, and music and visual art of a similar beauty, move me far beyond the limits of my customary rationality, so that I find myself in a realm where I find no difficulty in accepting both the existence of the paranormal realm and the eternal presence of God. In fact neither the paranormal nor the spiritual dimensions of reality can be 'proved' except by personal experience and the effect it has on the person's attitude to the great things of life, namely: our relationships with other people; integrity in monetary and other material dealings; generosity in spirit; and a willingness to sacrifice ourselves unhesitatingly for the sake of less fortunate brethren (who, as the parable of the good Samaritan points out, include everybody).

When the psychic sense acts in close collaboration with the spiritual dimension, it is greatly magnified, revealing the glory of the whole world. The Spirit of God sheds its light over the entire creation, thereby illuminating all that is hidden and occult. It is this type of psychism that is greatly to be sought, and has been the preserve of such great Christian saints as Teresa of Avila and Seraphim of Sarov. The more usual, mundane type of psychism that is associated especially with spiritualistic mediums is considerably less edifying. Some of the 'messages' come from indeterminate sources often purporting to have an exalted authority, while others may be demonic spirits impersonating the living dead. It is, of course, possible that some of the 'spirits' are really aspects of a surviving personality or even a total entity growing in the afterlife. The one aspect of by far the majority of spiritualistic communications is not their manifest demonic character so much as their almost unbearably repetitive triviality. The same conclusion comes to me as I read accounts of reincarnation as elicited by hypnotherapeutic techniques. Clearly if we are ever to know about the situation of the living dead, we will need to transcend the limitations of our own personality, with its typically selfish desire for reassurance that we at least are destined for immortality. It is no wonder that the Bible proscribes all occult practices. If we seek first the kingdom of God and his righteousness – which means setting our minds on God's kingdom and his justice before everything else – all the rest, including reassurances about the afterlife, will come to us as well (Matthew 6.33).

The test of a well-lived life on earth is our list of priorities. Those who devote much of their attention to the life beyond death, apart from specialist parapsychologists, show a distorted view of human priorities. If we cannot live our present lives satisfactorily in terms primarily of human relationships, it is vain indeed and almost terrifying at its worst to ponder over what may happen to us when we die. As mentioned in chapter 3, we make our future lives both here and in the life beyond death according to our present behaviour and our relationships with those who inhabit the world with us. The two sources from which psychic attacks on humans arise are hate-filled people and demonic entities which, in all probability, are the same as the angels of darkness that are recognized in all the world's religious cultures. In fact the ultimate agent of such an attack is always a demonic entity whether or not it works through the agency of a human intermediary. In this respect it is useful to consider the meaning and depth of hatred. It is a state of such emotional intensity that the normal intellectual capacity is completely overwhelmed by a negative, destructive power which, if unchecked, could destroy not only the person who is the object of the attack but also the one from whom the emotional discharge proceeds. Our own century has seen far too many examples of this mutually destructive tendency to require any further description.

But where does this destructive emanation arise? It comes from the combined forces of darkness that dominate the world, rather like the collective unconscious described by C. G. Jung. This darkness has a psychic origin, and its nature and purpose is essentially destructive. It works towards the destruction of all creation; its own will, which is limited in power and extent, is mastered by the human element. Here the will is much more potent, but the character considerably less vindictive. The combination of a malicious person and a demonic entity empowered by a dynamic will is a fearsome force to confront. On its own the emotional disturbance merely makes the individual feel discontented and out of harmony with the world around them. If they have good self-control, which is the most important quality of a properly acting will, the emotional effect will be recognized for what it is, and its charge used positively for work of a constructive nature. A good example of this 'sublimation' could lie in concerning oneself with the welfare of especially deprived individuals, provided this concern was not merely a mask behind which one may spread hatred against a particular class or group in the society in which one was working. In this respect the truly free will is the active manifestation of the true self, or soul, in the world at large. It is free inasmuch as it is attached neither to its own emotional needs of recognition by other people (to say nothing of material substance like food or possessions) nor paralysed by fear of rejection by its peers if they move in a different direction from its own way.

The evil that emanates from a destructive person is based on their attitudes, which are potentiated by demonic activity arising from psychic sources. Of the two negative powers, the perverted human will acting from a malicious personality is the more powerful. The demonic component is by contrast less strong, not because of its relative benignity but through its poor driving force. It is therefore always inadequate simply to blame a human crime or misdemeanour on to demonic activity. It is the human weakness that allows the demonic agent to produce its own baleful effects.

The destructive effect of a psychically evil or negative person affects the entire atmosphere of a place with a feeling of foreboding, that something very unpleasant is present and liable to strike at any moment. The usual physical signs of psychic attack may sometimes appear, but these are merely superficial events compared to the fear felt deeply in the soul. Sometimes the feeling of psychic malaise gradually lessens and the individual returns slowly to normal, but on other occasions the feeling of despair persists and can be the precursor of a mounting depression. The most unpleasant attack that can be mounted by a viciously motivated human under demonic influence is the effective curse, also called a malediction or an imprecation. This dramatic utterance may be a cry of fury in a situation where the person believes that they have been the victim of dishonesty perpetrated by an evilly motivated individual. The emotional response, which is a combination of fear and indignation, leaves them in turn particularly open to their own fear and indignation, and the result may be a terrified person who bears a grudge against a particular individual, or a racial or national group.

An outstanding group that is especially noteworthy in this respect are the gypsies. They are members of a wandering race (called by themselves Romany) of Hindu origin with dark skin and hair, living by basket-making, horse-dealing and notably fortune-telling, and speaking a much corrupted Hindi. Their paranormal powers are well known, and when people purchase their wares they are assured of good fortune. But, on the other hand, if no money is forthcoming, a curse may be laid on the head of an ungenerous person, and I have no doubt that on occasions misfortune, often associated with ill health, has followed such a curse, sometimes lasting for a considerable period afterwards.

This consideration gives rise to a number of problems. When a curse is laid, how much is its effect purely psychological? The power of 'suggestion' – which is really imagination (and as such is used widely by those who advertise their wares in the media of mass communication) – is enormous. The terrible effects of propaganda in our own hyper-civilized century speak volumes about the poor capacity of perception among those who are schooled in one way of thought to the exclusion of a broader background of experience. If a curse is laid upon the average person, its effects are bound to remain in the mind for some considerable time. Indeed, if the matter is dismissed too easily and rapidly, the superficiality of the mental and emotional processes are demonstrated, and this is not necessarily a good thing. No one is the object of a curse who has not aroused the burning hatred of the person who has uttered it. The individual should turn the matter over in their mind to see whether there is any attitude within themselves, to say nothing of any culpable action performed, that has occasioned this emotional outburst in the other party. It is clear that I regard most of the psychological damage effected by a curse to be at least primarily psychological, but where there is great hatred of a persistent character that has an inwardly murderous intent, I would see the person as being obsessed, or infested, by a demonic spirit of high potency that was using the person's psychic energy for highly destructive purposes. The matter as always is one of the will; if the individual's will is strong and free it will be able to withstand even the most vicious curse imaginable, but if there is no capacity to choose for oneself, one is all too easily liable to be taken over by an assembly of destructive agents from outside if the conditions are right for their emergence, and these may show themselves as a curse. Some people who are both powerful psychically and destructive emotionally can intentionally or even unintentionally lay a curse on some article of considerable sentimental or intrinsic value.

This thought reminds one of the teaching of some among the charismatic movement, which tends to sense the devil at work wherever things do not proceed as they would have them go. At present this type of religion is extremely powerful because its phenomena attract a wide sweep of people with such proceedings as healing 'miracles', speaking in tongues, collapsing on to the ground followed by a sense of deep peace and renewal, and the discernment of spirits. The discernment is closely related to the prior prejudice of the person. Thus the type of individual who is dedicated to a highly respected religious group is bound to be suspicious of all psychic communication, and quite rightly so from their point of view; the truth is completely contained in the precepts of their special faith, and anything outside its parameters is undesirable. People who are converted to a highly charismatic faith are strongly advised to destroy all objects claimed to lie under a curse, and I have known of a number of very painful incidents in which the misled victim of one of these fanatical groups, which I personally would have no compunction in describing as evil, has been prevailed on to sacrifice valuable property to the point of embracing severe poverty. The reason why I describe many such groups as frankly evil is because they are controlled by a master figure or figures that interfere with the lives of lesser members of the group to the extent that their own will is impugned. The freedom of the will is God's greatest gift to us, for we cannot even accept his love without choice and commitment. When a person leaves such a group in a brainwashed condition, they cease, at least temporarily, to be full humans.

It is interesting that the other powerful group that tend

to see, from time to time, curses around special objects, are the spiritualists. When one considers how diametrically opposed the ultra-religionists are from the spiritualists, one can only wonder how they have this quirk in perception in common. But there is a world of difference in attitude between the two. The religious group are motivated by fear (even if they stress that Jesus has attained the victory), which in its turn leads to hatred. This is the reverse statement of 1 John 4.18, which we have mentioned on a number of occasions, that perfect love banishes fear. By contrast spiritualism, for all its failings and illusions, is not demon-infested, even if practitioners can play unwisely with evil material and cause considerable damage. It is for this reason that I warn everyone against 'dabbling' in the occult, which includes the ouija board as well as spiritualistic seances. One never knows what one is dealing with, and the devil always has work for idle hands. It should be noted that 'charismatic' phenomena are manifestations of psychic power. This applies to the miracles of Jesus and the various Christian saints no less than to various psychic agencies, like, for instance, spiritualists and other practitioners of the occult. It is the character of the individual practitioner that tells us whether their employment of their psychic powers is selfish or altruistic. A healing ministry such as that of Jesus or one of the world's many saints (not necessarily Christian in name, but always Christian in selfless love and dedication to the highest that we humans can grasp) is a tribute to the psychic faculty at its highest.

It is when this faculty is misused to boost the personality or wealth of the practitioner or to denigrate all other ways to God except their own, that the psychic path becomes dangerous. One notorious way is that of 'black magic', in which the practitioner uses their power for purely selfish means, in the course of which anyone who gets in their way is summarily removed. Magic itself is best understood as the employment of psychic powers for purely selfish motives. It is called 'white' if the intentions of the practitioner are well meant, or beneficial for another person, but the more one thinks about the matter, the less proper does it seem to interfere with either the workings of nature or the benefit of a fellow human until or unless one's assistance is actively sought. I therefore have no sympathy for practitioners of magic, who, by the way, are not to be confused with stage performers. These merely use sleight of hand to entertain and bewilder audiences who meet in places of relaxation. The physical phenomena of mediumship such as materializations (the conjuring up of objects out of nothing, a particular phenomenon well described in India) need expert gifts of parapsychology to separate them from stage sleight of hand.

The whole field of psychism, and especially its alleged physical manifestations, is a paradise for the gullible individual, but the specialist usually needs little investigation to assure themself of charlatanism on the one hand or simply poor observation on the other. In parapsychological research it is well known that a psychic person performs better before a sympathetic investigator or group than in front of those who are naturally dismissive of the whole subject and automatically hostile to the individual. To me this stresses the close affinity of emotion and the psychic sense. In an aesthetic event like a concert, in which the psychic element is much less obvious, the performers are much more at their ease and play more satisfactorily if the audience is well disposed to them because of their love of music. The standard of performance is considerably lower if the audience is basically uninterested, and is wishing to leave the concert hall as soon as possible, perhaps to attend what they regard as more important events.

In my own experience, demonic attacks are liable to afflict three types of people: those who traffic unwisely in psychic matters, notably trying to make contact with the dead; those who use psychic means to predict the future or to do anything else for personal gain; and those who are afflicted with a malicious hatred against another person or group of people. If one is unwise enough to attempt to hurt another person psychically or by a curse, one thing is certain: the injury or curse is visited tenfold (metaphorically speaking) on a vicious or mentally disordered person. There is no mystery in this statement. Emotionally and spiritually whole people can reflect psychic ill will rather like a wall resists any missile hurled against it. Is it advisable to consult 'clairvoyants', people who are claimed to have precognitive powers? I personally cannot recommend such a course even if these claims are true. I believe God always leaves the choice to us, and that all things work together to good for those who love God (Romans 8.28).

The matter is stated rather nicely in Ecclesiastes 11.1-6,

Send your grain across the seas, and in time you will get a return. Divide your merchandise among seven or perhaps eight ventures, since you do not know what disasters are in store for the world. If the clouds are heavy with rain, they will shed it on the earth; whether a tree falls south or north, it must lie as it falls. He who keeps watching the wind will never sow, and he who keeps his eye on the clouds will never reap. As you do not know how a pregnant woman comes to have a body and a living spirit in her womb, so you do not know the work of God, the maker of all things. In the morning sow your seed in good time, and do not let your hands slack off until evening, for you do not know whether this or that sowing will be successful, or whether both alike will do well.

I would go even further in saying that most precognitive statements are unpleasant if they are factually true. They warn of imminent death or larger disasters of one type or another. It is very common for a 'sensitive' to claim to have had a premonition of a train or aircraft disaster which has resulted in a frightful toll of casualties. When the matter is investigated impartially it is usually found that the warning was vague and coloured by prejudice.

Demonic attacks on humans may show the character of

obsession, or infestation, and the much rarer but far more dangerous possession, but clinical depression is nearly always of a psychological origin. In the obsessive state, the demonic agent is in close communication with the human, but has not overwhelmed or 'taken over' its personality. There demonic infestation is associated with depression, a slackening of religious belief, and a general malaise that infects all aspects of life. The arts, media of mass communication, and even the sweet savour of food are deadened of all living interest. In fact, the afflicted person feels close to death, and the depression may on occasion almost make suicide appear a justifiable option. Once the demonic spirit is sent away from its present place of residence to the care and love of God, the mental and psychological condition of the afflicted person quite rapidly returns to normal. The way these symptoms differ from those of spiritual dryness is distinguished by their response to deliverance.

The important aspect of all deliverance work is to send the invading spirit back to God's care and not leave it unprotected in the general environment, where it can do great harm. I do not believe that either obsessing or possessing spirits are necessarily evil. They are always misplaced, and this is how they produce their baneful effects. If the spirit is intrinsically evil, it is obvious that its effects will be especially unpleasant on the afflicted person.

This is seen most dramatically in the rare state of true demonic possession. Here the personality is completely eclipsed by the spirit, and now it shows itself in a most alarmingly vicious way. The human victim behaves blasphemously, rejecting all traces of any previous faith and sneering at anyone who still holds on to it. There is preternatural strength, especially when they are in the process of being exorcized, and if nobody else is present to protect the exorcist during the grim procedure, they may be severely mauled.

Therefore in any 'major exorcism' it is most important that the minister be protected physically as well as spiritually by the prayers of the faithful, which are always essential in the ministry of deliverance. This is not a work of virtuoso psychic brilliance but of a group of devout Christians working together under the leadership of Christ.

Another phenomenon that is well recognized in people who are demonically possessed is a hyperacuteness of psychic awareness; they tend especially to exhibit clairvoyance. They may be able to recognize a person coming to visit them for the first time. Their manifestation is complete in its form even when they show themselves fully for the first time to be demonic spirits. One remembers the account of Jesus exorcizing demonic spirits from two possessed men inhabiting the territory of the Gadarenes. These spirits recognized Christ at once as the Son of God, and asked whether he had come to torture them before their time, requesting that if he is to drive them out, they may be sent into a herd of pigs. This dramatic narrative occurs in Matthew 8.28–34, and also in Mark 5.1–20 and Luke 8.26–39, in which latter two only one possessed man appears and the territory is that of the Gerasenes.

One might say in passing that incarcerating demonic spirits in an earthly domain can only be recommended as a transient place of rest (and safety for the rest of us). I would expect that those 'unclean spirits' were soon sent on to the full caring love of the Father. The removal of demonic spirits is an integral part of the healing ministry, because they transmit psychic debility which weakens the entire human organism. When Jesus performed a work of deliverance not only did he release the spirit from bondage to evil humans so that it could pursue its proper work as assigned to it by God; but he also removed a source of imprisonment from humans so that they could be free to realize their potential as sons of God, in imitation of the Son of God who shows us all the full meaning of wholeness, which is the end of the healing ministry. A demonic spirit is primarily alone, but can express its malevolence by being manifest, for example, in human company rather than by staying aloof.

Two Johannine statements attributed to Christ illustrate this full healing ministry: 'If you stand by my teaching, you are truly my disciples; you will know the truth, and the truth will set you free' (John 8.31–2), and 'I have come that they may have life, and may have it in all its fullness' (John 10.10). It is bondage to our lower nature, the repository of all that is selfish and unclean in us, that not only imprisons us by its own action, but also lays us open to demonic attack. Understanding this important truth and acting upon it will set us free in the way that Jesus indicates both by his teaching and in his life. Life and truth are inextricably bound together, and the uniting agents are love and courage. The love will make us open to all varieties of people so that we may serve them without preference. Courage makes us able to renounce all that is personally dear to us to the glory of all living creatures. In another famous statement of Jesus there is a union of life and freedom, love and truth. 'There is no greater love than this, that someone should lay down his life for his friends' (John 15.13).

We judge ourselves and are judged by others on our sequence of priorities. On what do we place the highest value in our life? Is it material security, the recognition of other people, the fulfilment of our native potentialities, or our prestige and significance in society generally? None of these is to be dismissed as merely trivial, for while we are living in the world we are bound to respond to its scale of values for our own education as well as to be of assistance to other people. Indeed, the more we understand what life is teaching us, the more do our own learning and the ability to help other people come together. The psychic realm plays an essential part in this education process, for when we are surrounded by spiritual entities of indifferent character, the more are we challenged to use our own powers of discernment and to rely less on the opinions of other people, especially on matters of a moral nature.

The evil aspects of demonic attack wreak their worst effects by breaking our own spirit, so that we become like whimpering children. We have to learn to overcome this innate weakness, this cowardly response that prevents us becoming full humans of the type promised by Jesus in John 10.10. If our trust is firmly rooted in Christ, our true representative of the Father in the world, we can, through no effort of our own, move beyond fear to a living faith that shows us eternity in a single glimpse. The nature of eternity is always love, in which there is no place for fear of any kind. Now at last our relationships with a vast variety of living beings, no longer restricted to the human species, can be consolidated, so that we cease to be childishly masterful and destructive, but become constructive and compassionate initiators of a new order of creation under the aegis of God. This is the way of love in everyday life and in the living world of universal harmony.

8

Conditions Mimicking
Psychic Assaults

———⸻⸻⸻———

It is by no means uncommon for a person to complain that they are being influenced by someone in close proximity to them. Not infrequently the invading agent seems to reside in the mind, or even the head, of the afflicted person. They beg for it to be removed, and will consult exorcist after exorcist to effect a release from this bondage. But it is obvious that whatever the nature of the focus, it does not appear to be a foreign entity, whether a discarnate human or a truly demonic spirit. It is here that psychiatric knowledge is very helpful, for in fact the unhappy individual is suffering from mental disease. The 'differential diagnosis' between entity attack on the one hand and mental disease, usually some type of schizophrenia on the other, can be very difficult, especially because most psychiatrists do not believe in psychic entities. These they would call various types of 'complexes' if they belong to psychoanalytic groups, or else manifestations of organic diseases of the brain if even theories that transcended brain function were dismissed as illusory. Since we are all working with material that has not been properly analyzed and is therefore subject to our own prejudiced judgement, it is extremely difficult to give definitive rules about the matter of diagnosis and therefore of treatment.

And yet having admitted such extreme agnosticism about the clinical evidence of psychic attacks as opposed to psychiatric or psychopathological manifestations, it is not always so difficult to distinguish between the two clinically. On the whole there is a greater disintegration of the personality where there is severe mental disease than when there is simply demonic infestation. The functions of cognition – namely, knowing, perceiving and conceiving – are interfered with to greater or lesser extent in mental disease, whether organic or psychopathological (some practitioners would see the two as a common whole). By contrast, cognition is better preserved during demonic infestation even if there is severe emotional imbalance and volitional disturbance (an interference with the working of the will). In fact, demonic attacks paralyze the will by virtue of the fear they induce, but in due course the psyche learns to accept the new situation, and then it may grow in the stature of greater health.

There are a number of varieties of schizophrenia, and that most likely to mimic a demonic infestation is the common paranoid type. In this condition, the person believes that they are under constant malign attack from a source deeply implanted within them. It speaks constantly to them, often giving questionable advice and information, and commanding them to perform various actions. Some of these may be deleterious to the person and destructive to other people. Paranoid schizophrenic subjects tend to believe that they are the victims of organized assaults from the dark forces both on the earth and in realms beyond the earth. The cause and mechanism of schizophrenia are still unknown, but a biochemical disturbance of the brain is favoured by many psychiatrists. Nevertheless, the chemical treatment of schizophrenia is not especially successful in many cases, though the voices the sufferers may hear so constantly may be considerably quietened so that there may be a degree of inner peace. At the same time the delusions (false beliefs and impressions) of persecution may also lessen, but there tends to be a residuum of auditory hallucinations (apparent perception of voices not actually present) and sometimes other hallucinations also, and also of paranoid delusions.

The question arises; are schizophrenic subjects more liable to demonic attack than the remainder of the population? My own impression is mildly to the affirmative, since on a number of occasions I have been able to lessen the severity of schizophrenia after deliverance work. But on no occasion have I been able to effect a cure of the mental disease. Practitioners, always unorthodox in my experience, who claim cures of schizophrenia after their deliverance work have always been proved at the very least to be premature in their judgement and at the worst pure charlatans. In this respect it is always important to understand that quite a number of factors are involved in the genesis of mental disease. These include hereditary predisposition; brain damage from such disparate factors as birth trauma, accidents later on in life and malnutrition; various inherited disorders of metabolism that affect the brain as part of the body as a whole; vascular disease affecting the blood supply to the brain; and brain tumours; and no doubt other factors which a specialist in the field of neuropathology would enumerate in a trice. Usually a person is referred by an observant doctor to a minister of deliverance when the symptoms do not tally with those of well-recognized mental disorder. I hope this type of collaboration may come more into its own in future.

Another disease of the brain, but not a mental condition, that may reproduce some of the phenomena of demonic attack is temporal-lobe epilepsy. In right-handed people, it is the right temporal lobe that is affected in the classical syndrome: there is a brief lapse of consciousness followed by an alarming period of spatial and/or temporal dissociation. With spatial dissociation there is a period during which the person does not recognize their usual surroundings and lives in a world of their own imagination (usually decidedly unpleasant), while the temporally dissociated person is oblivious of the present time, living once again in a private world. The attack, like that of epilepsy generally, does not last long, and then there is a very rapid return to customary consciousness, but a residual sleepiness may last for a little while. If the left temporal lobe is affected in a right-handed person, there is a more typical epileptic fit with shaking of the right side of the body, biting of the tongue, and a transient lapse of consciousness. In neither of these two types of 'partial epilepsy' is there prolonged unconsciousness, foaming at the mouth, or spontaneous evacuation of the bowels or bladder, such as occurs in a classic epileptic fit.

At one time, epilepsy was ascribed to demonic possession. It was also called the 'sacred disease' inasmuch as it was held that the sufferer was being acted upon by some holy force from on high. It was at the time of Hippocrates, who lived between 430 and 357 BC, that this view was first queried, and a cerebral origin of the condition accepted. Nevertheless, there is at least one healing miracle of Christ in which a demonic spirit is blamed: a boy with a severe epileptic fit from whom Jesus exorcized an attacking entity (Matthew 17.14–20 with parallel passages in Mark 9.14–29 and Luke 9.37–43). To attribute this miracle to a demonic agent being exorcized would be derided as primitive superstition nowadays, and indeed we know that there is a disturbance of function of part of the brain during a fit. There are a number of effective anticonvulsant drugs that can usually control the epileptic tendency in predisposed subjects; a far more predictable way than any form of spiritual healing, including that employed by Christ himself. However, the drugs simply keep the tendency to fits under control. If they are cut down the fits will almost certainly recur, and therefore anticonvulsant therapy is nearly always a lifelong necessity. When Jesus performed his miracle, were the effects likewise temporary, or did he effect a permanent cure? If the relief was indeed permanent, something more must have been done than merely expelling a demonic spirit; the brain itself must have been healed. It should incidentally be noted that the basic cerebral defect underlying the epileptic state is still not understood. It could well be that a demonic assault could precipitate a fit in a previously predisposed person, a reflection underlining the view that many conditions affecting living animals have a multiple causation.

Severe states of depression have been attributed by the sufferer to demonic attack. The person feels a destructive presence around them which seems to afflict them bodily as well as mentally. Sometimes this attack of depression follows a severe emotional battering. Perhaps a personal relationship has gone wrong and there is a feeling as if a curse has been laid on them. This state can resemble the very serious clinical depression that may precipitate an attempt at suicide in a very disturbed person. On other occasions everything seems to go wrong in a person's life, and they long either for relief or else oblivion. Although it is plausible enough to attribute this situation to the assault of the devil, it is in fact a disease of the brain, like schizophrenia probably due to a biochemical defect, and often greatly relieved by contemporary drug regimes. Indeed, drug therapy has been more successful in the treatment of depression with or without mania than in any other mental disease. This does not, incidentally, mean that every case of depression will automatically have a favourable outcome but simply that there is often hope at the end of the tunnel.

Anxiety states may sometimes be precipitated by fears of demonic attack; the human power of imagination can be very strong. A strong religious faith can sustain the individual through this and other mental disturbances; on the other hand, there are other religious practices that lead to darkness rather than to light. Certainly the metaphysical beliefs of a strongly psychic person play a sometimes decisive role in their mental processes no less than their bodily health.

A final thought on the subject of demonic infestation and evil actions comes in Matthew 10.28: 'Do not fear those who kill the body, but cannot kill the soul. Fear him rather who is able to destroy both soul and body in hell.' The interpretation of this terrible passage is far-reaching. The only One who can in fact kill the soul (in hell or anywhere else) is God, for under his law the soul is naturally immortal. Thus if one begins to fear that one is close to total destruction of the personality, one's awareness of guilt must be overwhelming. In my opinion this is a very serious result of a poor religious education acting on a disordered mind, for even as noxiously destructive a person as Hitler must have had some strong reason for his racist views. The uncomfortable suspicion remains that the dark, demonic forces can use the holy name as easily as the blessed one in heaven (see Matthew 4.6 for the devil using the very words of Scripture in attempting to entice Jesus into displaying his spiritual charismatic capacity for purely egoistical exhibition). What matters with all charismatic, psychic powers is the use to which they are put. The more ego-centred, the less does the person give lovingly to serve the world with their God-given capacities. The snare attached to all psychic capacities is the self-importance they offer the gifted individual, making them feel a cut above humanity at large. This temptation is held out through their unusual gifts that certainly strengthen the thinker's suspicions that the nature of reality is considerably vaster than the materialist would have the world believe.

The exegesis of this passage is very disturbing, since only God can destroy the soul in hell or anywhere else, and under his law a soul is naturally immortal and incapable of being destroyed. A fear of absolute destruction of the personality which is controlled by the divine grace stresses a total imminence of complete punishment for wrongdoing. It to my mind suggests a pathologically guilt-ridden conscience.

9

Deliverance of Demonic Agents

————

The essence of deliverance is to determine whether a disturbing agent is the cause of the attack, and if it is demonstrated that the attack is due to a demonic agent, to deliver it as soon as possible to God's care. It is here that meticulous discernment is essential, and this is a rare gift. It is God-given as a special grace. This rare gift of immediate psychic awareness is a true charism, or spiritual gift, given by God directly for a special purpose. It differs considerably from the rather crude psychism so common among those who have no use for their gift other than that of acquisitiveness. The truly charismatic ('spiritually psychic') type of person can enter more directly into the Divine Presence, and ask God essential questions about the sufferer's condition, whether there is a strong psychic link or whether it is purely psychological. If it were merely psychological, no amount of exorcism would be of any use, and would indeed be counter-productive, stimulating additional fear and mental disturbance. If, on the other hand, there was clear evidence of psychic invasion, either acting alone or in association with a psychological problem, it would certainly be worthwhile delivering the invading spirit, whether human or demonic, to God's care both for its own progress and for the relief of its human captive.

Using one's own psychic gifts, one may move in what

appears to be the right direction, but the way is hazardous and not infrequently distorted by prejudice on the one hand and demonic interference on the other. I am always wary when people proffer their advice, often completely unsolicited, about psychic matters. To me it seems usually like the blind leading the blind. In such a case I would hint at a demonic source meddling with the life of an innocent person through the interfering zeal of an exhibitionistic individual. If we were fully Spirit-directed people, by which I mean fully directed by the Holy Spirit, we would be shown the answer, or perhaps what was right for us to know about the answer to a particular spiritual problem afflicting us, or someone else we were seeking to help. We would then have the discretion to use our God-given knowledge wisely and with humility. This wisdom and humility are, however, products of long experience of life lived among many different types of people; so much so that a single life on earth seems hardly adequate. Here, however, we approach the possibility of multiple lives on earth (reincarnation) or somewhere else in our vast universe. This view of the progress of human life after the death of the physical body is strongly opposed by the world's major theistic religions, at least in their orthodox form, but the wider encompassing faiths of the East have considerably less difficulty with it. All we who are sensibly uncommitted on this issue can store it away as a possible explanation of the soul's growth into spiritual understanding in eternity at the present moment in time.

When I am involved in the work of deliverance I admit my own ignorance, and enter into deep prayer. This does not mean, at least as far as I am concerned, addressing God in a long conversation, for he knows both my disposition and the source of my request far better than I do myself. The reason for my certainty in this matter is absolutely clear to me, because I believe that God has chosen me for this work (originally with my friend Geral) quite specifically, and the directive to do the deliverance comes from him and not primarily from the victim. Nor am I the prime

mover in deliverance work, because I find it quite exhaust-
ing; and also not a little frustrating if the person does not
play their part later on. If the work goes well one soon
becomes widely known, as Jesus was. I believe that the
exhaustion that comes from a celebrated deliverance ministry like his could have explained some of his irritation
when called on to treat the daughter of the woman from
Syro-Phoenicia described in Mark 7.25–30. In any form of
healing ministry it is most important to emphasize to the
person being treated the necessity of constant prayer, so
that they may always be open to the life-giving power of
the Holy Spirit. There is in fact only one 'healer' and that
is the Holy Spirit, who is also responsible for the work of
deliverance.

When I pray at any time I give myself entirely to God
whom I worship with rapt devotion, just as if he were a
person close to me, but I do not visualize God in any form.
Even the personal pronoun 'he' is quite inappropriate to
what I feel about the Divine Identity, but in the end one
is obliged to use some form of words to describe the
Intangible. When my mind is completely clear of all intrud-
ing thought – a state of awareness that comes after years of
quiet, undisturbed, devoted meditation – I am aware of an
emptiness which contains the totality of creation and at the
same time transcends it and time itself. This emptiness or
void is the nearest I can get to describing God to another
person. But the emptiness or void is not merely without all
worldly attributes; it is also the apotheosis of all that exists,
and in it pure undemanding love is experienced. In this
respect, true love seeks nothing for itself, but is fulfilled by
seeing the beloved full of grace and joy. In the end the
beloved is all-inclusive, as St Paul was saying in a somewhat
different way in 1 Corinthians 13. It is impossible to define
the nature of God in purely legalistic terms inasmuch as
love is both personal and transpersonal. By this I mean
that love is concerned with the individual creature no
matter how humble it may appear.

On the other hand, love is not restricted by the needs of

individuals to the exclusion of the greater whole, of whom
each individual makes their own claim and contribution.
When I enter the silence of eternity I come close to the
person who claims my help, and I bring them to the Divine
Essence in which all inadequacy is filled with love. It is this
love that gently but authoritatively removes the demonic
spirit from the human soul and brings it to God's healing
care. What I am trying to say is this: in my exorcism work
I do not use personal power to overcome something threatening and potentially evil; instead I lift the spirit to the
knowledge of God's undemanding love, compared with
which all other considerations are trivial. To quote once
more 1 John 4.18, 'Perfect love banishes fear', inasmuch as
the demonic sphere exerts its baneful influence by the
fear it inculcates. This fear is real enough on a material or
intellectual level, for here there are constant barriers to
full communication with other individuals, but on the level
of the Holy Spirit we are all one, the good and the bad
alike. The Holy Spirit breaks down all illusions of separate
existence, inasmuch as we are all the children of God, the
unpleasant no less than the pleasant. By our tendency to
judge uncharitably, we play an important part in erecting
barriers so that we tend to fight against our fellow creatures.

It therefore follows that a helpful ministry of deliverance
is quite as concerned about the welfare of the invading
agent as it is about that of the person. In my experience the
invasion is much more likely to be due to a misplaced
spirit than to one that is frankly malicious, and even if
the spirit is apparently evil, who are we to judge its nature
or its origin? All comes ultimately from the Divine Source,
and there will be no peace in the world until it is directed
thither. The work of exorcism gives one a supernatural joy
as one contemplates the end of creation. One is never far
from Julian of Norwich and her *Revelations of Divine Love*,
in the thirty-second chapter of which she is told by God
that all will be well. This is much more than reassurance
for neurotic people; it reaches the very depth of the human

condition. Julian was shown that the Divine Concern reaches out not only to the great and noble but also to the lowly and simple creatures. Even more important than this is the revelation that no matter how evil the deeds may be or how great the affliction produced, there will be a time of relief and understanding for everyone no matter how badly they have behaved. The love of God would never consent to the total damnation of any creature, but some mysterious deed would be performed at the last which would bring all creatures into the heavenly grace. These would include the fallen angels, the heathen, and those who, though they have been baptized, have lived un-Christlike lives and so did not die in a loving state.

The nature of this great deed was not shown to Julian, but she was urged to follow the larger way of universal faith while remaining loyal to the teaching of the universal Church. This is certainly the ideal solution to a theological dilemma where dogma clashes severely with universal love, and only a great soul can venture along this path by paying due respect to both of them. Intense faith is the essential quality required, and this is one of love's most precious gifts. To know this love, all one has to do is to remain perfectly calm and open to the present moment. This is a true counsel of perfection, for how can a normal person possibly remain calm in the presence of something so terrifying as a demonic spirit? And yet, as long as one's trust – a more explicit word than faith at least in this context – remains pure and open, one is available to the healing energies of the Holy Spirit, and then events may occur that could seem miraculous to the agnostic onlooker. Much of my own healing ministry has been conducted in this way: medical and spiritual practice work together hand in hand. The quality required both of a minister of healing and one who is capable of being delivered of a demonic spirit is complete humility. The doctrine of Mark 9.33-7 is compelling:

So they came to Capernaum; and when he had gone indoors, he asked them, 'What were you arguing about on the way?' They were silent, because on the way they had been discussing which of them was the greatest. So he sat down, called the Twelve, and said to them, 'If anyone wants to be first, he must make himself last of all and servant of all.' Then he took a child, set him in front of them, and put his arm round him. 'Whoever receives a child like this in my name,' he said, 'receives me; and whoever receives me, receives not me but the One who sent me.'

When I do an exorcism I enter into rapt prayer with God, whose nature is, as far as I am concerned, pure love, and I let that love permeate every fibre of my being. I know the rapport is as perfect as it can be, remembering that I am an imperfect mortal, when I cease to be aware of myself except in the role of servant, and then a marvellous joy illuminates my mind as I recognize my Creator and a wordless dialogue takes place. Into my mind flow the needs of many people whom I know, most often with illness. In my non-interfering concern, the power of the Holy Spirit can be broadcast on to all I remember in my prayer. My own view about the efficacy of prayer is that it should be available to everybody, by virtue of the divine love that has no favourites. Therefore in my intercessions, while I necessarily have to limit their scope and number to a relatively few people and causes, I have no doubt that the power of my prayer has a vaster range than this. As St Paul puts it, 'Then have done with falsehood and speak the truth to each other, for we belong to one another as parts of one body' (Ephesians 4.25). The love of God can never be limited to the few except by their own choice, and even this choice is cleansed of all fear and doubt by the experience of love in everyday life.

The procedure I adopt is very similar to that I use in dealing with unquiet spirits that I described in chapter 4. I first say the Lord's Prayer and then the Collect for the direction and guidance of the Holy Spirit. I then enter into profound imageless contemplation, so that the love of God can permeate my whole being. In this state I can address the Divine Essence with relevant questions without any emotional barriers, whether doubt, fear or awe. God does not need even our awe, what is required is quiet obedience in a state of complete trust.

The questions I address are whether there is a demonic source causing the disturbance or if the problem is associated with the unquiet spirit of a dead person contaminating the psychic atmosphere of a habitation where it once lived. If I was shown that neither of these possibilities fit the case, I would then enquire whether the problem was essentially psychological. In this case exorcism would be categorically ruled out, and counselling with psychotherapy would be recommended. In this respect we remember how severe psychological problems, especially in adolescent subjects, can occasionally produce poltergeist phenomena (see chapter 3). If I merely ask the questions in the air, as it were, I am likely to receive a reply that is equally insubstantial, and heavily tinctured by personal prejudice. It is for this reason that I always cringe from exorcists that cast a baleful eye over people of whom they so clearly disapprove for personal reasons that are much more related to enmity than demonic infestation. To know oneself is the prerequisite of all spiritual service, and the number of such practitioners is small on the ground. While some people seem to have a natural self-awareness, the majority learn this by bitter lessons of humiliation and pain. When one has been divested of much personal illusion of importance, an interesting awareness dawns on one. It is one's own egoism that blocks out the radiance of the eternal moment, and when that ego-centre is displaced, a new world of meaning and relationships is uncovered. When one has attained this knowledge – a combination of divine grace and enlightened will – the previously invisible opens up to clear visibility, and one can see that which is barely visible to most of one's peers. The emphasis on grace cannot be overemphasized, for one cannot see beyond the world of the senses with any degree of reliability in any other way.

The most controversial part of my deliverance ministry is the use of some object to confirm the information I have received inwardly. I have already described this practice in a previous book, *Angels: Messengers of Grace*. I use a coin that I have blessed (and continue blessing for all fresh deliverance work), and toss it on to a carpet, having made a compact with God beforehand. If it turns up 'heads' the answer is 'yes', while 'tails' signifies 'no'. It is surprising how much criticism such a practice has occasioned among some people who are alarmed at my superstition, gullibility, or even lack of basic spiritual discernment. Oddly enough, I agree with all these criticisms. The procedure may indeed be interfered with by a demonic agent or more simply a trickster in the psychic realm. On the other hand, a more rationalistic type of critic would have no great difficulty in showing that the results of such a test were purely random. Nevertheless I press ahead despite the barrage of discouragement around me. If the result is positive, I send the entity, whether demonic or human, to the divine care; whereas if it is persistently negative, it is evident that the person requires psychological help. I do not follow the indication of a single 'coin test' unless it is already inwardly clear to me, but I rather 'challenge' it in the name of the Lord Jesus Christ. Not infrequently there is indeed a change in the indication, so that I can act accordingly – usually performing an exorcism. When the work is over, I test once more to be sure that the entity has been delivered to God, and here the coin test is again invaluable. This test is admittedly crudely pragmatic but it continues to support me in my work.

The basis of this test is thoroughly biblical: the use of sacred lots. In the severe reverse that the Israelites suffered before the inhabitants of Ai, which we mentioned in chapter 6, Joshua was instructed by God directly to find out who had brought the divine displeasure on the people. Only the total destruction of the idolator and his family would relieve the situation, after which the Israelites could continue their triumphant occupation of Canaan (Joshua

7.13–25). Another example of the divine disapproval involved Saul and his son Jonathan. Here King Saul had issued a curse on the man who took food before nightfall and before he had taken vengeance on his enemies, and now when he consulted God through sacred lots he could not get any reply. It transpired that Jonathan, Saul's favourite son, had disobeyed his father's command, and eaten some honey on the tip of his stick. Saul threatened to kill Jonathan, but his men forbade this. In this way Jonathan was delivered, but Saul broke off the pursuit of the Philistines (1 Samuel 14.24–46). The New Testament also has several references to trial by sacred lots. For instance in Luke 1.9 it is recorded that Zechariah, who despite his old age, was to become father of John the Baptist, was chosen by lot, by priestly custom, to enter the sanctuary of the Lord and offer the incense, while in Acts 1.23–5 Matthias was chosen by lot to fill the place left empty after the villainy and appalling death of Judas Iscariot.

If my ministrations produce no observable effect on the coin test, I submit in prayer. If the person is severely disturbed I celebrate the Eucharist without delay: the presence of other devout Christians is in any case of the utmost value and should always be sought, though sometimes this may be a counsel of perfection in a basically unbelieving community. Much of my work is done at a distance from the afflicted person as I described in chapter 3, and I have found no oddity in celebrating a Requiem Mass for such a human entity over the telephone with the person who is caring for them making the accustomed responses. When one can accept the natural immortality of the human soul, it becomes easy to pray for anyone, whether alive or dead as we understand these terms. Prayer is simply bringing the love of God to the individual for whom we are concerned. In this way an earthbound spirit, whether demonic or human, may be released to God's care and love.

Therefore I command a demonic spirit to leave this earthbound plane and go to that place in the life beyond death which God has prepared for its reception and healing. In this work my helper, Geral, whom I have mentioned already (and died four years ago) and I work in close collaboration. The work is far too dangerous to be conducted alone, but unfortunately there are few who can contribute their share to it. That I continue my deliverance work with my beloved helper Geral who died four years ago can hardly avoid disturbing some readers, but the fact remains that her living soul works in close contact with my own. As I quoted earlier on in chapter 2: 'Many waters cannot quench love, no flood can sweep it away; if someone were to offer for love all the wealth of his house, it would be laughed to scorn' (Song of Songs 8.7). The command is firm but not hectoring. These are the words I use: 'In the name of God the Creator, God Most High, God the Father, God the Son and God the Holy Spirit, Geral and I command you demonic spirit to leave here, and proceed to that place in the life beyond death which God has prepared for your reception and healing.' After a brief period, I repeat the formula, this time bidding the demonic spirit to leave here 'and this earthbound plane' instead of simply 'here' as in the first command. After a few more seconds I repeat the formula a third time, bidding the demonic spirit to leave here 'and proceed to that place in the life beyond death that God has prepared for your reception and healing, there to do the work for which you were created'. I end each command with the instruction, 'Go in the name of God the Father, God the Son, and God the Holy Spirit.' After the third command I remain absolutely quiet for a short time, and then I free the spirit (no longer demonic) from all obedience to evil humanity, in this respect remembering that perverse humans are much more dangerous than spirits because of the limited capacity of the demonic will compared with the strength of the vicious human will (see chapter 7).

No demonic spirit could equal a Hitler in destructive power because the spiritual realm is not imbued with hatred and similar negative emotions to anything like the same degree as is encountered among deranged people. Therefore it is inadequate to blame demonic spirits for anti-social or criminal human conduct. Free will is God's most precious gift to us, and we misuse it to our own, and the world's, peril. The spirit world can imbibe the fruits of that evil and the results accruing from it; it is in this way that the spirits can become demonic if they have a natural ambivalence to evil actions. The spirits of light (the bright angels) are always near to the Divine Source, and bring the love and enlightenment of God to the world. Thus do the spirits of good and evil work with humans, but I believe, following Dame Julian's 'revelations of divine love', that in the end all will be well. I would be prepared to go even farther than this, and affirm my conviction that the evil impulse is also as near to divine will as is the good, inasmuch as it provides us with the experience of the manifold aspects of life, without which we would remain like self-centred children. But this is a hard doctrine, and one more palatable to the type of person who has suffered terribly in the course of their life on earth and has come through with the fire of love blazing in their heart. These are the true saints of humanity.

After having freed the spirit I wait a short time, and then say the Lord's Prayer, after which I repeat the coin test. I ask whether the spirit has been satisfactorily delivered into God's care. If the answer is positive (and I am inwardly satisfied) I thank God in a prayer of thanksgiving. If the result is negative, I repeat the test in the name of the Lord Jesus Christ (the challenge I have already referred to). If the result now reverts to positivity, I repeat the challenge, and if the second test remains positive I accept that the spirit is now in the divine care. If the result remains negative, I likewise repeat the challenge, and if there is no change, I accept that my work has effected no deliverance. I am usually 'told' to be patient, and repeat the procedure on the following day. This was the way Geral and I were encouraged to continue. In fact some loosening of the attachment was effected by this preliminary work, and subsequently the spirit could be delivered to God. The same principle applies to discarnate human entities who will prefer to remain where they are rather than move on to God's care in a wider domain (chapter 3).

Assuming the spirit has been delivered into the divine protection, I demand of the person whom I have helped that they lead a regular prayer life and pursue regular Bible reading according to some accredited lectionary. If this discipline is not pursued with devotion, seeing it as the most important work in the person's life, reinfestation is very likely to occur, and the last condition of the person could well be worse than the first (Matthew 12.45). I lay great stress on the Eucharist also, but the person should be acquiescent to its use and meaning. None of these measures and sacraments are helpful if the recipient is not educated with regard to their sanctity; they simply become objects of superstition. The use of holy water, sprinkled on to the person or the premises they occupy (or both), is a much recommended practice. The sprinkling is called 'asperges', and the brush and other implement used for the sprinkling is called an 'aspergillum'. I personally have not found this an especially helpful addition to my armamentarium of prayer, direct deliverance of the invading spirit, Bible reading, and the Eucharist, but I would not discourage anyone else from using this aid.

Where do the demonic spirits then proceed? I believe they are enveloped by the love of God to be healed of their perverse tendencies, often manifestations of weakness rather of defiant will such as not infrequently encountered among recalcitrant humans. As I have already speculated, some of this evil may have been acquired from human sources. I believe that evil humans proceed likewise to God's protecting love and care, but here the situation is complicated by the powerful human will which can at least theoretically disregard all God's offers of healing and reparation. The tragedy of the Israelites, as recounted in the books of Hosea and Jeremiah, was their total rejection of the divine offer of forgiveness and succour until destruction by the Assyrians and the Babylonians respectively was quite inevitable. Fortunately a 'remnant' was preserved, which, at least after the Babylonian exile, was permitted to return to their homeland. I believe that a similar situation may occur in the life beyond death, except that here the disobedient human will come, at least in the great majority of cases, to their senses fairly rapidly. The utter desolation of a self-imposed hell, where one is out of communion with one's fellows indefinitely, soon turns one to divine assistance, and one is shown in firm kindness where one has transgressed and what is the proper way of progress in the life beyond death. The demonic spirits are delivered to God once they have been freed by specially gifted human agents (those with psychic sensitivity together with profound spirituality), but the human soul, having far greater autonomy, has to play its part by 'purporting an amendment of life'; in other words changing its entire way of thinking and style of living, as I have already indicated in relation to people who have been delivered of demonic spirits.

The exorcism of unclean localities, usually polluted by evil people possibly living many years ago (perhaps even centuries), is carried out in a similar manner. First I try to ascertain the source of the trouble – it is usually a recent corrupting influence – and then I use the formula of exorcism to move it onwards to divine assistance. It is most important to ascertain whether living agents are involved in the problem, since there can be no permanent clearance until these are either removed or else exorcized. Furthermore, exorcism is seldom successful in a living person if they are not cooperative. Therefore surreptitious deliverance techniques are not to be recommended. Sometimes a locality may be the seat of an annoying disturbance that does not have the undertones of the frank malice of a demonic spirit.

I am alluding here to a mischievous entity, and in my deliverance formula I use these words after the Lord's Prayer and the Collect for the direction and guidance of the Holy Spirit and the ensuing preamble: 'I command all demonic and alien spirits and mischievous entities to leave here and this earthbound plane, and proceed to that place in the life beyond death that God has prepared for their reception and healing.' I have learnt over the years that not all invading spirits are by any means intrinsically evil, but are simply interlopers who have lost their way and in their unaccustomed position can be a considerable nuisance. Some of these spirits are merely strangers, but others also have playful tendencies that can cause confusion. But they should all be sent to God's care without delay. Some of the effects of these misplaced spirits can resemble poltergeist phenomena, but the circumstances of the appearance usually give a ready clue about their origin. They are not especially related to adolescent people or other psychologically disturbed folk, and a psychically sensitive person can effect a communication with them through prayer and loving concern.

It is probable that most psychically infested localities have been subject to human contamination. I do not know whether a locality could have been a spontaneous nidus for spiritual entities apart from human contamination, but I do know that the human provides a remarkably hospitable seat for entities to spread their malign influence. It is the undisciplined nature of so much human activity that is the focus of the trouble, while the perverse will can permit a host of evil to pervade the psychic atmosphere. It follows therefore that until humans grow up emotionally and learn spiritually, the world will continue to be a residence of an array of psychic entities ranging from the demonic to the alien and the merely mischievous. These will work hand in glove with deranged people (deranged in mind and soul), and cause immense havoc. St Paul expresses some of these thoughts in Romans 8.14–25:

For all who are led by the Spirit of God are sons of God. The Spirit you have received is not a spirit of slavery, leading you back into a life of fear, but a Spirit of adoption, enabling us to cry 'Abba! Father!' The Spirit of God affirms to our own spirit that we are God's children; and if children, then heirs, heirs of God and fellow-heirs with Christ, but we must share his sufferings if we are also to share his glory. For I reckon that the sufferings that we now endure bear no comparison with the glory, as yet unrevealed, which is in store for us. The created universe is waiting with eager expectation for God's sons to be revealed. It was made subject to frustration, not of its own choice but by the will of him who subjected it, yet with the hope that the universe itself is to be freed from the shackles of mortality and is to enter upon the glorious liberty of the children of God. Up to the present, as we know, the whole created universe in all its parts groans as if in the pangs of childbirth. What is more, we also, to whom the Spirit is given as the first fruits of the harvest to come, are groaning inwardly while we look forward eagerly to our adoption, our liberation from mortality. It was with this hope that we were saved. Now to see something is no longer to hope: why hope for what is already seen? But if we hope for something we do not yet see, then we look forward to it eagerly and with patience.

When I meditate on this solemn but joyful passage my inner views are confirmed: God is the only as well as the supreme source for all the good and evil in creation. It seems that the function of evil in our lives is – by throwing us into confusion, pain and suffering – to cause us to move beyond the enclosed complacency of a safe, pleasant and sheltered existence in a full understanding of the nature of ourselves and our fellow creatures. 'To know all makes one tolerant (*Tout comprendre rend très indulgent*)' is a universally known saying of Mme de Staël. This type of universal knowledge comes through a courageous encounter with the darkness as well as the light of creation, so that in the end we can say with Terence, who lived from 195 to 159 BC, 'I am a man, I count nothing human alien from me (*Homo sum; humani nil a me alienum puto*).' Evil is therefore not to be removed so much as to be transfigured into a creation of light.

In cleansing psychically, the concern of the human agent is vitally important, because the powerful human will acting in a beneficial way initiates the process in the right direction. As we noted in chapter 2, God needs us as much as we need him for the work of creation, a work that has no ending until the end of time. It is no exaggeration to assert that evil influences emanate primarily from human sources, at least in our universe. On the other hand, the four cardinal virtues of justice, prudence, temperance and fortitude are combined with the three theological virtues of faith, hope and charity; and help cleanse the psychic atmosphere, and bring the indifferent psychic fraternity back to creative action. We may 'pick up' emotional malaise from psychic sources, but rather than wallow in our gloom it is our duty to lift up the darkness to God's healing care by the practice of assiduous prayer. This is in fact our constant healing work on behalf not only of our fellows but also of the entire universe, which, as, as we remember 'up to the present . . . in all its parts groans as if in the pangs of childbirth'. This prayer will serve not only to heal the darkness in which we live, but also our own darkness, so that we may be cleansed of our vices and live instead in the joy of the sacrament of the present moment. If only our eyes could be focused on the wonder of life around us, we would move from the prison of the self to listen 'while the morning stars sang in chorus and the sons of God all shouted for joy' (Job 38.7).

10

Preventive Measures against Demonic Attack: Good and Evil Influences

————~~~RR℗ARR~~~————

The surest prevention against demonic attack is living so wholesome a life that one is well protected from adverse elements in the psychic atmosphere. This is not to be equated with separating oneself from all temptation and living the life of a holy recluse. Was not Jesus himself tempted on three occasions by the devil just before his ministry commenced (Matthew 4.1–10)? Only when he had passed the test did his ministry proceed. The temptations in the wilderness that confronted Jesus were in the first place psychic: turning stones into bread; and being set on the parapet of the temple in Jerusalem, from where he was challenged by the devil to throw himself down. Finally the devil took him to a very high mountain, and showed him all the kingdoms of the world in their glory. He promised to give all these to Jesus if he would only fall down and do him homage. Jesus rejected all these demonic overtures, saying 'Out of my sight, Satan! Scripture says, "You shall do homage to the Lord your God and worship him alone."'

Had Jesus submitted to any of these challenges, he would

have demonstrated his psychic mastery to his rather
gullible contemporaries, so that they might well have
bowed down to him as a 'master', and he would automatically have assumed superiority over them simply by virtue
of his psychic gifts. He could have assumed the character of
a monster just as easily as that of a saint. How indeed do
we distinguish between a 'psychic genius' (often an evil
genius) and a saint? The clear indication is the way of Jesus
as compared with that of his adversaries. He was full of
love and compassion, but never sentimental or blurring his
inner vision with personal sympathies or intolerance. He
spoke what he thought. The tirade – against the scribes
and the Pharisees because of their gross religious
hypocrisy – that occupies most of Matthew 23 gives a fine
picture of Jesus dealing with the important members of
the Jewish community, while instructing the crowds that
gathered around him and also his disciples. This is the way
to prevent demonic attack both on ourselves and on other
people also. The question is always the same: to what do
you bow in greatest allegiance? Is it your own good (seen
on an inevitably selfish basis) or the benefit of your fellow
creatures? If the latter, you are very close to God, for in
him alone there is both personal peace and service to your
fellows. When we have made this choice categorically and
are prepared to assail the long trudge before us with faith
and iron determination, only then can we triumph over the
subtle demonic forces that confront us day by day. Only
now can we consider something greater than merely our
own advantage, and move on with joyous abandon into a
greater work for our fellows under the aegis of God. The
closer we are to his presence, the more protected we are
from demonic assault.

He who lives in the shelter of the Most High, who lodges
under the shadow of the Almighty, says of the Lord, 'He
is my refuge and fortress, my God in whom I put my
trust.' He will rescue you from the fowler's snare and

from deadly pestilence. He will cover you with his wings; you will find refuge beneath his pinions. His truth will be a shield and buckler. (Psalm 91.1–4)

A parallel view is, 'God is our refuge and our stronghold, a timely help in trouble; so we are not afraid though the earth shakes and the mountains move in the depths of the sea, when its waters seethe in tumult and the mountains quake before his majesty' (Psalm 46.1–3). This famous psalm rejoices over a river whose streams bring joy to Jerusalem, the holy dwelling of the Most High, for God is in her midst. She will not be overthrown, and at the break of day he will help her. Psalm 46 goes on to remind us that nations are in tumult and kingdoms overturned, for when God thunders the earth melts. The psalm exults in the Lord of Hosts' intimate presence, for he is our fortress. And so comes the zenith of this magnificent psalm, 'Come, see what the Lord has done, the astounding deeds he has wrought on earth; in every part of the wide world he puts an end to war: he breaks the bow, he snaps the spear, he burns the shields in the fire. "Let be, then: learn that I am God" ("Be still, and know that I am God", is the more familiar Authorized Version of the Bible translation), exalted among the nations, exalted in the earth. The Lord of Hosts is with us; the God of Jacob is our fortress' (Psalm 46.8–11).

One cannot, however, neglect the obvious fact of widespread warfare in the world despite God's power to influence events in the many remarkable instances of divine intervention, when all seemed lost and the power of civilization seemed to be falling irretrievably into the hands of evil people and criminals. A third psalm that asserts God's transcendental power and purpose is the finest of all, namely Psalm 23; its greatness lies in its beauty and simplicity. 'The Lord is my shepherd; I lack for nothing. He makes me lie down in green pastures, he leads me to the water where I may rest; he revives my spirit; for his name's sake he guides me in the right paths. Even if I were to walk through a valley of deepest darkness I should fear no harm, for you are with me; your shepherd's staff and crook afford me comfort.' The Lord spreads a table for his beloved in the presence of his enemies, and has richly anointed his head with oil, so that his cup brims over. Goodness and unfailing love will follow him all the days of his life, and he shall dwell in the house of the Lord throughout the years to come.

It is evident from the content of psalms such as these that closeness to God's presence serves especially well to separate us from the 'prince of the world', which is a characteristically Johannine way of describing the devil (John 12.31; 14.30; 16.11). The question arises as to how much we ought to be completely isolated from baleful influences. If a complete spiritual quarantine is imposed between the devil and his courtiers and ordinary people, there will be no meeting of minds and therefore no growth in knowledge or sympathy. If we mix only with those whom we like and admire, we will become increasingly static in our sympathies and attitudes. The devil and his entourage bring us to less pleasant aspects of reality, including especially those characteristics within ourselves that often lie hidden from our own inner sight, though ridiculously apparent to those around us. There are two main ways of preventing demonic attack against us: surrounding and isolating ourselves against all harmful influences – rather like immunization against infectious diseases in a large, drifting community – and developing spiritual power to combat evil directly by confrontation. In fact, the first way can have only a limited effect, for no scheme of personal isolation has any hope of permanence. But as we begin to develop our own spiritual resources from inside ourselves, so there arises a focus of spiritual power that can drive off all psychic evil and eventually become a zone of intense spiritual light, which is the way we recognize the Divine Presence.

We have already considered the unquiet dead as a possible focus for demonic activity or, to be more accurate, discarnate activity. We described this matter in chapter 3, but it becomes really important when it involves people who have died as accident victims, or foetuses who have been the subject of abortions. As a rule, the younger the victim of 'unnatural death', the more unsettled is its soul, and the more disquietitude does it set up. There are basically two varieties of abortions: the first is described as 'inevitable' and is due to some abnormality in the mother or the foetus; whereas the second is 'induced' and is due to some mechanical interference between the foetus and the mother. In neither instance is the foetus well disposed after its rejection and death, for it tends to remain in psychic attachment to its mother, and sometimes to other members of its family also. There is often a great degree of resentment inasmuch as the foetus has lost its foothold in the family circle, and it may intrude quite disastrously in the family proceedings until it is persuaded to move on to God's care, a circumstance extremely unlikely until a great deal of explanation and apology has been paid to the discarnate entity. A book published some thirteen years ago called *Healing the Family Tree* and written by Dr Kenneth McAll (Sheldon Press, an imprint of SPCK, 1982) discusses this matter rather more fully.

In my own experience the troublesome entity is usually a dead foetus, but sometimes it is a considerably older child who was related to the family, and occasionally there does not appear to be any family connection between the young child and the group to which it has connected itself. In such an instance I would suspect that the entity became united to the welcoming family group shortly after its detachment from a rather unfriendly discarnate fellowship. One thing is obvious to me: there is no absolute rule concerning the fate of discarnate entities that have not been attached to their family tree. When an unquiet spirit has been apparently causing trouble, it is first important to draw up a family tree to see if there is any obvious source of the trouble. When the possible cause of the disharmony has been unmasked, I speak firmly to it, advising it to move onwards to the light where God's love is encountered. Quite often such a scheme of progress seems to be perfectly adequate, but if I sense any reluctance to go forward, I celebrate the Eucharist at once, either in the home or just as effectively in a church. Occasionally I celebrate Holy Communion over the telephone, as I mentioned in chapter 4, or I say a more solemn Requiem Mass according to the circumstances of the case. In all this work the departed soul is brought close to God's presence and love, and then I believe it is set free to proceed with the work lying ahead of it, perhaps the deliverance of all who were in bondage to the malicious intent of demonic entities.

The bondage of the departed lies in the realm of an inability to forgive past hurts, something we all have to experience in the vale of purgatory, where we are taught both to forgive others and to pray to be ourselves forgiven by those whom we had treated meanly when we trod the painful course of the world's deceptive ways. We remember the electrifying sentence of the Lord's Prayer in this respect, 'Forgive us the wrong we have done, as we have forgiven those who have wronged us' (Matthew 6.12). Jesus proceeds to elaborate on this teaching:

> For if you forgive others the wrongs they have done, your heavenly Father will also forgive you; but if you do not forgive others, then your Father will not forgive the wrongs that you have done. So too when you fast, do not look gloomy like the hypocrites; they make their faces unsightly so that everybody may see that they are fasting. Truly I tell you: they have had their reward already. But when you fast, anoint your head and wash your face, so that no one sees that you are fasting, but only your Father who is in secret; and your Father who sees what is done in secret will give you your reward. (Matthew 6.14–18)

This exposition of the Lord's Prayer puts the concept of protection against evil psychic influences in a very positive light. In fact, we cannot obey this beautiful advice all on our own, because we shall very soon be assailed by the demons of fear on the one hand, and vicious anger on the other. We remember once again the warning of 1 Peter 5.8-9, 'Be on the alert! Wake up! Your enemy the devil, like a roaring lion, prowls around looking for someone to devour. Stand up to him, firm in your faith, and remember that your fellow-Christians in this world are going through the same kinds of suffering.'

Some people have a natural psychic sensitivity. They tend to be self-effacing, a not very surprising trait when one considers the generally hostile approach of the materialistic masses that dominate the current intellectual scene. Meanwhile the simple soul who is decidedly psychic finds it most comfortable to hide their gift, until they are the subject of so severe a paranormal experience that they cannot keep it to themselves any longer. ('Paranormal' is a synonym for psychic, just as parapsychology is synonymous with psychical research.) They seek any intelligent help that may serve to elucidate their problem, or to indicate how they may proceed with their strange gift to their own advantage and the benefit of other people. They will find, in our destructively agnostic age, that most authorities in the realms of psychology and education tend to disregard all 'occult' phenomena. Some will regard these as mental aberrations, while staunchly religious people are more likely to see the finger of the devil in it all. It is bewildering how quite innocuous occurrences can assume demonic proportions in the minds of pious people who fear rather than love God. Surely the Most High is the master of all that is, seen and unseen (according to the Nicene Creed).

If one's criteria illuminating the fullness of proper living are centred around the Divine Presence and all that pertains to it, one need fear no evil because a mightier protection is at work within us, and even if we are assailed by evil of the most brutal kind, we may call on the Divine Name in serenity for protection, and we shall be comforted (which is an archaic word meaning 'protected'). We are shown the way to move onwards even in the face of terrifying demonic energies, most of which have been unleashed within ourselves by forces from outside our recognition. These 'psychic energies' within ourselves are concentrated in focuses called 'psychic centres'. I knew about them even when I was a small child and far distant from any source of occult lore. They are related to our external anatomy rather than to our inner organs and their physiological connections, but of their linkages to our intricate system of spiritual connections I have never had any serious doubt. In the Indian (Hindu) tradition these centres are known as 'chakras', a Sanskrit word meaning wheels, because clairvoyant practitioners claim actually to see whirling wheels of psychic energy coursing over the points of psychic communication. I personally know of the existence of the chakras by virtue of what I have experienced in my own body, but I have never seen anything of what I have described either in myself or in anyone external to me.

The value of knowing about points of psychic communication is their relation to the ministry of healing. It can be well worthwhile to lay one's hands over those points of the body where a major chakra is known to be present. This is especially true in relation to the situation of the accepted points of the body's psychic energy. These are (a) around the umbilicus or navel; (b) over the front of the heart; (c) over the front of the throat; (d) over the bridge of the nose between the eyes; and (f) on the vertex, or top, of the scalp. By placing one's hands over the appropriate psychic centre in a person in pain or discomfort in a nearby area of the body, one may often afford relief which may last for some time, but it must always be stressed that in a condition of severe disturbance orthodox medical investigation dare not be ignored.

Two points arise from this interesting discussion. First, not all psychic phenomena are *ipso facto* deleterious; on the contrary, some may undeniably be beneficial. Apart from a healing energy that may flow from them, they may be a means of precognition, clairvoyance and telepathy that could afford the recipient important information about private or future events that might influence the course of their later actions. As I have mentioned, one should not seek auguries from afar, but when they appear to be given spontaneously, they need not be cavalierly dismissed. It is better that they should be thoughtfully and seriously considered, small though they may appear to be. Every phenomenon in the world has its own significance, and if we are wise, we 'fill our thoughts with these things' (Philippians 4.8).

The second point concerns the fundamental difference between Eastern and Western concepts of human nature, and therefore psychology. The Eastern view is essentially holistic, by which I mean that it tends to regard the person as a complete unit: body, mind, soul and spirit. The body is the external form of the personality by which we function in the world; the mind regulates and governs the body's activities; the soul is the seat of our deeper value judgements, especially those appertaining to moral and aesthetic matters; whereas the spirit is the seat of action of the Holy Spirit within us, and therefore our means of knowing God as St Paul puts it – 'Christ in you, the hope of glory' – in Colossians 1.27.

Although the philosophy underlying complementary medicine is more typical of the East than of the West, there are some well-recognized unorthodox therapeutic systems of the West also. A classical example is homoeopathy. Here a minute dose of a drug, infinitesimal in amount, that in larger quantities would have the same general affect as the condition from which the patient was suffering, is said to have a completely paradoxical power of healing the condition itself. The preparation has no noticeable physiological effect in a much larger dose, and it is believed that the infinitesimal 'potency' is the basis of the drug's action. The principle underlying homoeopathy was discovered by a

German physician called Hahnemann who worked about two centuries ago, but like so much therapeutic practice of the East also (China and Tibet no less than traditional Hindu therapeutics) its mechanism is obscure to the point of absurdity to the downright Western mind.

This works according to rational principles: various remedies have a predictable response. If they are given in the recommended dosage the anticipated response may be relied on. Too small a dosage will have no effect at all, whereas too large a dose will probably produce toxic effects. The standard dose may occasionally have an unusual response due to allergy (or hypersensitivity), or simply as a result of idiosyncracy, which may be defined as a completely unique effect of a drug on a person's metabolism, which manifests by producing a totally unexpected sequence of signs or symptoms. Apparently the patient reacts unusually because of some inborn error of metabolism. As we saw earlier on, predictability is the basis of the scientific method, and parapsychology has yet to fulfil its criteria. The same criticism applies to the traditional medical practices of India, China or Tibet but, on the other hand, numerous individuals have benefited from their ministrations. It is believed that the infinitesimal 'potency' is the basis of the homeopathic medication's action. If this is true, it would seem that the action of the preparation is primarily psychic, by which it influences the mind and the body, while, at the same time, enabling the person to be more open to the Holy Spirit also; indeed a truly holistic approach to personal healing and health.

I believe that the response to Eastern medicine and homoeopathy is largely idiosyncratic: some people are amazingly benefited, whereas others remain unaffected. A particularly well-known homoeopathic remedy is called arnica; it is often remarkably useful after severe injuries where there has been considerable bruising. It also relieves the pain. An unusual healing practitioner of recent time was Rudolf Steiner. His system, called anthroposophy (in contrast to theosophy, another branch of the occult founded by Madame Blavatsky and Annie Besant) includes very erudite teaching about the nature and continuation of the soul after the body's death. He also had healing and clair-voyant gifts, and his system of therapeutics shares points in common with herbal medicine. A completely different approach to complementary medicine is acupuncture, which is very much a Chinese speciality. The practitioner may deduce many aspects of the patient's condition by simply feeling the pulse, but what is ascertained bears little corre-spondence to the orthodox medical approach known to a doctor or a nurse. There are mysteries here that are available only to those long schooled in these arcane, traditional practices that involve diagnosis as well as treatment. Chinese medicine works more on a system of bodily meridians than on chakras, but I suspect that both are mechanisms of bringing body and mind into psychic equilibrium, from which the Holy Spirit can proceed and perform its trans-forming function in our dense physical body. I visualize the psychic realm as a vast flowing river that carries all the sediment of our earthly life on its crest, where it is carried to the healing light of the Holy Spirit. The darkness is transfigured into the uncreated light of God in whose presence everything can be renewed and redeemed.

Another aspect of alternative medicine at present in vogue is reflexology: the soles of the feet are massaged quite vigorously according to a way that identifies various parts of the foot with a corresponding area of the body. I would guess that the sensitive parts of the foot are stimulated and this effect is transmitted to the major chakras, espe-cially the one over the bridge of the nose and that over the vertex of the skull. Not only is the body irradiated with healing energy, but it is also laid open to the power of the Holy Spirit. The Hindu healing exercises of Yoga work not only through the muscular development they engender, but also from the full application of the body, mind and psyche to the knowledge of God, using the concept of knowledge in its Johannine sense.

Therapeutic relationships contain the material of their healing potential, because in this type of relationship there is a fine transference of psychic energy from the one person to the other. As such, transference has long been recognized as the real basis of healing in psychotherapy, but in fact the work of transference and counter-transference is much more radical than merely a transmission of emotional energy from the analysand to the analyst. It is fundamentally a release of psychic energy from the soul with its locked-up store of scarcely tolerable suffering to the therapist, who is able to bear this immense burden after having been trained to come to terms with their own inner wilderness. In the same way, true friendship is shown by the capacity of people to bear each other's pain.

We have also to be aware of how easily we may be drained psychically by those who cling unmercifully to us, perhaps by making us feel ungrateful for some minor favour they did on our behalf in the past. A guilty conscience towards this type of person can easily mount into a similar feeling towards God. Therefore we should be aware of the natural selfishness that we all share while alive in the flesh. The first great commandment – loving God with all our heart and mind, soul and strength – should always precede the second one of loving our neighbour as ourself. Once we feel easy in our conscience towards God, we will find an equal ease in our conduct towards our fellow creatures. No human has the right to dictate our responses either to them or to the world at large. Freedom is God's supreme gift to us, but we have to learn how to use it with wisdom and a determination to be of use to our fellows. Those who become entangled with psychic groups are very likely to compromise their own integrity of action, and if an individual member strives to break free, they are held back by the threat of occult attack should they accomplish their purpose. Much of this is pure superstition, comparable to the circulation of chain letters with the threat that anyone who destroys the nasty missive and severs the link will have their subsequent share of personal misfortune. In fact, there are seldom any repercussions following the destruction of chain letters, and those who compose them are often the ones in need of medical treatment.

All this helps to assess the membership of a group, whether a church of acknowledged integrity or some occult society. Do they leave their members free to go elsewhere for friendship and further enlightenment, or do they cling doggedly on to them, preventing their growth in the freedom of full experience which is God's gift to us all? If the latter is the case, they are in the grip of an evil force which is intent only on their destruction as independent individuals. An obvious advantage of these fascinating complementary therapeutic systems over the hard-hitting rational approach of the West is their gentleness (on a systemic level) and paucity of obvious side effects. But it seems to be an invariable rule of life that nothing which is effective is without its own dangers and disadvantages. If one becomes obsessed with practices of psychic potency, one is liable to depend on their efficacy and the practitioners who prescribe such methods. I believe that the potency of unorthodox methods of healing generally depends on the relationship between the patient, the 'healer' and the remedy. I hearken back to Ecclesiastes 4.12, 'If anyone is alone, an assailant may overpower him, but two can resist; and a cord of three strands is not quickly snapped.' What I am saying here is distinctly the converse of the wisdom writer's dictum, for he is writing from a position of growing strength, while I am striving to lessen the power of outside agencies, so that the individual may establish their independence from external sources as they move into their way of life unimpeded by their past history of powerlessness. Therefore, if orthodox medical treatment leaves the patient dependent on a single line of therapy, which may ultimately be left behind, the complementary approach leaves him or her more or less permanently part of a patient-healer-medication team, which could be increasingly undesirable if the healer assumes the mantle of irreplaceable psychic virtuoso.

This is, incidentally, the problem confronting all relationships of dependency in which a master figure becomes established in the mind of the patient, or client, to use a term which has established itself in psychotherapeutic circles. This psychic dependency is seen to its maximal effect in the relationship between a medium and their supporters in an established spiritualistic group. But its unhealthy effect can also be encountered in groups practising reflexology and acupuncture. Therefore the psychic dimension is like a double-edged sword. Its power moves beyond psychic phenomena to embrace both emotional attitudes and spiritual aspiration. But its close connection with the demonic realms shows how unwise it is for anyone who is unschooled to dabble in these matters. The story of the sorcerer's apprentice told by Goethe and set as a magnificent tone poem by Paul Dukas reminds us how dangerous it is when powerful forces, whether scientific or occult, are placed in the hands of an ignoramus; in this case a sequence of words that activate broomsticks to bear water at the sorcerer's command. While he was in charge, all went well, but when the sorcerer went away for a time, the apprentice took over, and nearly caused a tremendous flood, which was obviated by the sorcerer returning just in time, and stopping any further movement of water by the broomsticks. The unfortunate apprentice had learnt the words to command the water to be brought, but he had not acquired the balancing knowledge of restraint.

Exorcisms should never be carried out except by devout Christians, since there is a great power that emanates from the holy name. This is stressed in Acts 19.13–20, in which instance some itinerant Jewish exorcists tried their hand at using the name of the Lord Jesus on those possessed by evil spirits. The evil spirits repudiated the authority of the exorcists, attacking them quite unmercifully almost to the point of their death, so that they ran out of the house battered and naked. In this particular case only one evil spirit caused trouble, but in many other instances there has been a veritable hive of demonic activity. The mention of believers who had previously practised magical spells is also significant; they collected the offending books and burnt them publicly. In such ways as these the word of the Lord showed its power, and spread more and more widely and effectively.

But as I have stressed so often in these pages, merely putting on a Christian front does little good. It is the inner disposition of the heart that alone matters; if this is truly God-centred, we will never be overcome even when we appear to be surrounded by all the forces of the universe. The psychic mode is also the place of illusion, which masquerades as reality because of the spectacular phenomena that may emerge from its orbit, but if we are patient and wait prayerfully we shall be shown the way past illusion to the foothills of divine grace.

11

Psychic Relationships: Befriending the Spirits

It is the psychic element of the universe that binds us close together in a mutual regard that far transcends all intellectual understanding but, as we have repeatedly stressed, not all these elements work to our benefit. Some are deliberately hostile, while others interfere with our own sense of dignity by clouding our discretion. So much of a free person's life is an experience of pain and frustration, and psychic illusion can easily lead us into escaping from these negative

Psychic relationships include two separate issues: relationships between entities, and their relationship with us. I have purposely avoided their relationship with other forms of life because this is basically contingent on our relationship with our fellow humans, with the world and with God.

> We love because he loved us first. But if someone says, 'I love God,' while at the same time hating a fellow-Christian, he is a liar. If he does not love a fellow-Christian whom he has seen, he is incapable of loving God whom he has not seen. We have this commandment from Christ: whoever loves God must love his fellow-Christian too. (1 John 4.19–21)

It is the psychic element of the universe that binds us close together in a mutual regard that far transcends all intellectual understanding but, as we have repeatedly stressed, not all these elements work to our benefit. Some are deliberately hostile, while others interfere with our own sense of dignity by clouding our discretion. So much of a free person's life is an experience of pain and frustration, and psychic illusion can easily lead us into escaping from these negative emotions into an easy, hospitable way of existence in the shallows of selfish concern. Indeed, psychic illusion acts by conjuring up spectacular visions that lead us along attractive paths which induce a state of self-inflation both by themselves and by stimulating us to seek the type of company that inflates our ego-consciousness to the extent that we lose sight of the way God has intended us to follow.

If we lose the way into an easy life, nothing seems to happen, but in fact there is a diminution in our complete psychical stature that may be the precursor of our cognitive collapse, similar in its own way to the atrophy of the body and mind of an aged person. Just as our best way to delay physical atrophy is by frequent bodily exercise, so the way of spiritual youthfulness is by meditation and prayer and by concern for other people. Indeed, personal health and sensible concern for those less fortunate than ourselves form good criteria for knowing how well we are serving God in the world. By sensible I mean a concern that does not put our own well-being under unnecessary risk – remembering the second great commandment, 'You must love your neighbour as yourself' (Leviticus 19.18). We are not expected to make martyrs of ourselves, for self-imposed martyrdom is an unpleasant emotional trait that has nothing to do with the spiritual life.

The question remains: how do we try to reconcile the beneficent entities that propagate peace and goodwill with their malicious counterparts that are intent only on the destruction of the true, the beautiful and the good? Experience over the years has taught me that the first requirement for a healing relationship is a naked determination to confront the adversary directly, so that complete candour can be established between the opposing factions. This is scarcely possible in an atmosphere of distrust, and indeed we have first to confront our own motives squarely with as complete an honesty as we can muster. If we were acting to destroy a human adversary, there is a considerable likelihood that we should fall disastrously under their system of defence, for they, after all, are acting only to pre-serve their own life. The same principle underlies our spiritual conflicts both with our fellow humans and the greatly magnified forces on the other side of life, which we call death.

When we find ourselves confronted by an enormous human figure like the legendary Samson (Judges 13–16), our courage seems to drain away from us, and we run for help to God, or to some equally powerful figure if we are unbelievers. But this so-called God is largely a figment of our imagination, and we are well advised to escape from his alleged power. In fact his real power shows itself in preventing us from growing into mature adults who can put our trust in our own powers and gifts. These are aspects of our own personality, and when they are courageously explored, we can begin to know the divine power within the soul: Christ in you, the hope of glory (which we have mentioned very frequently, and St Paul stresses in Colossians 1.27).

Another approach to discerning the right type of spirit is contained in 1 John 4.1–3:

> My dear friends, do not trust every spirit, but test the spirits, to see whether they are from God, for there are many false prophets about in the world. The way to rec-ognize the Spirit of God is this: every spirit which acknowledges that Jesus Christ has come in the flesh is from God, and no spirit is from God which does not acknowledge Jesus. This is the spirit of antichrist; you have been warned that it was to come, and now here he is, in the world already.

In 1 John 4.4–6 we read further,

> Children, you belong to God's family, and you have the mastery over these false prophets, because God who inspires you is greater than the one who inspires the world. They belong to that world, and so does their teaching; that is why the world listens to them. But we

124

belong to God and whoever knows God listens to us, while whoever does not belong to God refuses to listen to us. That is how we can distinguish the spirit of truth from the spirit of error.

This is what ought to be the essence of orthodoxy, at least in its religious connotation, the holding of correct or the currently accepted opinions especially on religious doctrine. Its converse is known as heterodoxy or heresy, but it may be merely original or independent-minded views or opinions that in a more hospitable climate of thought would prove to be quite acceptable to a large number of people. How then do we know whether we belong to God or merely to the world? The answer is clear to me: by the presence within our soul of the Spirit that animates us as it did when Mary, the mother of Jesus, greeted Elizabeth. When Elizabeth heard Mary's greeting, the baby in her womb leapt for joy (Luke 1.39–45). This is how I know that I am in the presence of God in whom I know the true, the beautiful and the holy. This last word speaks to me of moral and spiritual perfection, consecrated and sacred, and belonging and devoted to love. It is a shame that the word 'orthodox' conjures up a vision of narrow-minded, bigoted, self-sufficient people who have no doubt that the entire gamut of spiritual truth not only lies within their grasp, but is also unobtainable from any other source. One of the principles of this book is to attempt to demonstrate that the Most High works in many different ways – whether in psychology, religion or healing – and those of us who are wise accept all these indications of divine grace as special gifts to us in our travail and worldly disillusionment. But this travail and worldly disillusionment is also our personal pilgrimage to God, a pilgrimage like all others that is pursued in the company of many other seekers and yet at the same time completely alone. The depths of the soul contain our own secret known only to God, and our work is to unravel and elucidate that secret. Most of us seek rather to escape from the threat of loneliness by affiliating ourselves with other people and their points of view rather than facing the threat with its distant view of inner integrity.

There are two basic ways of confronting reality: one looks for safety and assurance, and the other for adventure. In fact all life is a type of adventure whether we accept the proposition or not, for we are here to grow into useful, experienced members of an adult community who are capable of tending to the needs of the rest of the living society. These in turn minister to our own concerns. St Paul expresses it memorably in Ephesians 4.25, 'Then have done with falsehood and speak the truth to each other, for we belong to one another as parts of one body.' To those who are psychically aware, this communal sensitivity extends both to the blessed angels and the great fellowship of saints that were at one time living in the world alongside us, and are now a permanent feature of the cosmic landscape. A saint is a member of the blessed community, one who identifies truth with the knowledge of the Most High and acts accordingly. In our world of phenomena it is comparatively easy, and satisfying too, to classify the spiritual powers according to our value judgements. This is how humans have judged members of their own group for many ages. Those who meet up with our inner spiritual requirements have been accorded the accolade of acceptability, whereas those who do not meet our needs are rapidly rejected. The acceptable spiritual entities have succeeded in bringing us closer to the presence of God within us, whereas those that are unpleasant have dulled the vision of God in the soul. This they do by filling us with negative emotions like fear, boredom, mistrust, hatred and destructive passion. A particularly destructive passion goes under the name of love, but in fact it is very similar to the movement that a python demonstrates as it embraces its victim in its lethal coils of destruction. This type of love is content with little else than the entire body and soul (if it could claim this also) of its victim. This is the essential difference between the ever-enduring love of God and the transient passions of some humans who almost carelessly abuse the sincere concerns of those in whom a chord of sympathy has been stretched. When they cannot lay claim to the person's complete identity, they recoil in anger.

In the end, the totality of spirits in the cosmos need to be brought together and reconciled, for otherwise spiritual warfare will persist indefinitely with each side claiming its superiority both in terms of strength and usefulness. Moral purpose can be largely ignored in respect of the demonic spirits inasmuch as they are motivated by self-interest which they tend to equate with using other entities for their business. The relationship between the darker side of the psychic dimension and the selfish aspect if human nature needs no further amplification. We in our simplicity may be misled into blaming the spirits for our difficult character traits, but in fact we likewise play our part in their misdemeanours. I have on more than one occasion emphasized that the emotional power inherent in the human will can immeasurably potentiate the negative psychic powers of the demonic spirits. But now I can stress a more positive aspect between the human-demonic relationship also. If we as humans actualize the divinity within us, so we can quite unconsciously begin to convert the world from darkness to light, from hatred to love, from negative thinking to positive activity. We do not plan this mode of approach intellectually; on the other hand, the love flows from us as we begin to care for other people.

In the first case, our concern is limited to only a few people, perhaps indeed only one, but if we are quite spontaneously prepared to sacrifice our time, energy and material resources for their wellbeing, so a flow of love may be initiated through the psychic realms which may in the end clear up the debris of misunderstanding, mistrust and jealousy, and bring many hostile entities or forces closer together. It seems scarcely credible that so lowly a creature and one so capable of terrible crimes as the human has also been granted the power of bringing divine love into the universe, when they forget their own sordid interests and begin to care for something greater than themselves. 'There is no greater love than this, that someone should lay down his life for his friends' (John 15.13). This love does not end its work when the friends are healed of their particular impediments; on the contrary, it only really starts to manifest itself at that point. The reason for this dramatic increase in magnitude is the capacity of love to grow in power and effectiveness when it is ever more widely dispersed throughout the universe. Just as we become most isolated when out of fear we separate ourselves from the main thrust of life (which, threatening though it so often is, remains the only way of maturing into a full adult stature in the present world), so self-giving love abolishes our isolation.

In a human situation, the truly destructive person is the one who is mentally or emotionally unbalanced to the point of willing the annihilation of all that exists, and the same line of reasoning applies to demonic entities also. Most are not nearly as destructive in intent as this, but are in a condition of confusion: 'Father, forgive them; they do not know what they are doing' (Luke 23.34). To this confusion is added a mischievousness and a state of general ill will. Since the demonic powers are present in a cosmos that God has fashioned, they dare not be ignored even when their actions and general attitudes are totally unsatisfactory in terms of the development of the universe into a Garden of Eden. Instead we should pay heed to Isaiah 30.15,

> These are the words of the Lord GOD, the Holy One of Israel: In calm detachment lies your safety, your strength in quiet trust. But you would have none of it; 'No,' you said, 'we shall take horse and flee.' Therefore you will be put to flight! 'We shall ride apace,' you said. Therefore swift will be the pace of your pursuers! When a thousand flee at the challenge of one, you will flee at the challenge of five.'

This oracle was spoken by Isaiah during the threat of an Assyrian invasion of Judea during the cruel and destructive reign of King Sennacherib, who descended from the north with his hordes of soldiers. If only the Israelites had put their trust in the Lord, all would have gone well for them, but, as usual, the human element had to be in charge! And so the Israelites preferred to seek an alliance with Pharaoh, for here was tangible strength rather than a glory that could not be described. 'What is seen is transient, what is unseen is eternal' (2 Corinthians 4.18).

Surely the most challenging demand in the Sermon on the Mount is contained in Matthew 5.38-48. Among other things we are enjoined not to resist anyone who does us wrong, but rather to turn and offer our left cheek if the right one has already been slapped. In the dispute that follows being sued for one's property, one should be prepared to give more than merely to stand solidly behind one's rights. In the same spirit, if someone in authority presses one into service one should go further than the demand. Give to anyone who asks, and do not turn your back on anyone who wants to borrow. Even more radical than this advice, we are told to love our enemies and pray for our persecutors. This injunction embraces something more than mere detachment; love will alone suffice. But how can we in all integrity love the unjust person who passes on their way through power irrespective of the permissibility of the demands? How can we in all sincerity love our enemies? None of this can be done purely by an act of will, for in such an attitude we would immediately reveal our spiritual superiority over our adversary, thereby evoking jealousy in those places where goodwill ought to prevail. Few attitudes are more insufferable than assumed moral superiority, because it puts the other party in a position of weakness which all the strength in the world cannot rectify. It is much better to confess our mortification when we feel we have been let down or betrayed by the other party. In the combined emotional mélange of wounded pride, disgust at the dishonesty of our fellow humans, and a general rejection of the concept of God, we may attain a deeper stillness than is usually our wont, and in this wordless silence our ears may be opened to the greater truths of the universe.

We may, for instance, see in greater depth how small our part in the world's economy truly is, and how much more we can play our part constructively by remaining quiet and listening with the inner ear to the voice of God within the soul. In this attitude of spiritual truth we are much more likely to become attuned to various spiritual entities ranging from the morally illiterate to the frankly demonic. Furthermore, in this experience of inner truth we can both be cleared of spiritual illusion (that we are special in the eyes of God) and an expectation that we should receive special recognition for our own work. The reward for seeing our work well done is a glow of happiness replacing the previous gloom in the face of a sufferer. To be able to give is our greatest privilege in this life. When these basic spiritual truths can be broadcast to the demonic spirits they may take heed and, despite their perennially bad humour, begin to change their attitude. 'Come for water, all who are thirsty; though you have no money, come, buy grain and eat; come, buy wine and milk, not for money, not for a price. Why spend your money for what is not food, your earnings for what fails to satisfy? Listen to me and you will fare well, you will enjoy the fat of the land' (Isaiah 55.1-2). In other words, the only convincing way to bring a recalcitrant member of a community to the love of God and their neighbour is by an attitude of selfless devotion to them and through them to the whole community.

Since we are indeed belonging to one another as parts of one body (Ephesians 4.25), we only begin to attain our own usefulness to the whole when we forget our individual parts as separate servants and work towards the common good. We are paradoxically most liberated when we have been able to cast aside our own self-importance. It is then that we can begin to see our own reflection in the faces of all who surround us as they in turn can see themselves in us. 'When I was a child I spoke like a child, thought like a child, reasoned like a child; but when I grew up I finished with childish things' (1 Corinthians 13.11). It is this process of mental maturation that so sharply distinguishes us humans from our more humble animal brethren, and I suspect the same is true of the lower demonic spirits also. Whereas the bright angels are eternal spirits acting to guide creation to the ways of God, the dark spirits accompany us on our way, teaching us to protect ourselves through the course of a dismal night of suffering through to the dawning of a new day. As we noted earlier in the chapter, our first duty is to take care of ourselves, for only then can we love our neighbour effectively also. Of course, our way of action does not end at this point, for we have to give ourselves fully as servants of the created order, and it is in this respect that the spirits of light illuminate our way forward.

When the spirits of darkness will have completed their part in our education into full living, they too will assume something of the light pouring from our bodies, and order will have emerged from our present chaos. 'While the course of the righteous is like morning light, growing ever brighter till it is broad day, the way of the wicked is like deep darkness, and they do not know what has been their downfall' (Proverbs 4.18–19). In the end the way of the wicked is their own judgement, for the darkness is what we know as hell, an atmosphere of meaningless isolation devoid of any fellowship. When the folly of the spiritual warfare they have occasioned among themselves as well the other creatures of the universe has been fully shown to them, I could envisage a complete change of perspective comparable to the change of heart that we all know within ourselves when our heart is open to truth far beyond the narrowing intellect.

We begin to live when we no longer need to attain the victory over our adversaries in order to prove our strength or superiority. If a victory is really important, its end should not have an eye to our own gratification, but that virtue should prevail and evil be thwarted. This attitude is in line with being the Lord's servant, completely open to his workings and putting up no barriers (Luke 1.38 and Isaiah 6.8–9 are good examples of dedicated service to God). While the life of the Holy Spirit is not lived for individual reward, its harvest is immortally enumerated in Galatians 5.22–3: 'Love, joy, peace, patience, kindness, goodness, fidelity, gentleness, and self-control'. When the psychic atmosphere of the universe has been lifted up beyond personal desire to a concern that all creatures may be saved in their eternal form, the praise of the heavenly host around the shepherds at the time of Jesus' nativity will have been fulfilled: 'Glory to God in highest heaven, and on earth peace to all in whom he delights' (Luke 2.14).

12

A Summing Up

There are several ways of communicating with each other. Direct verbal communication is explicit and intelligible, but there is also implicit communication, whether emotional, intellectual or psychic. Direct communication is soon recognizable through the effects it produces on our feelings and minds, so that we become enlightened by the knowledge and the impact that the information has had upon us. We indicate our response in our attitude and behaviour, so that soon no one can remain oblivious of the consequence.

The psychic way of communication is typically implicit, for here the details are largely implied but not directly or plainly expressed in terms of reference that may be immediately accessible to everybody. Psychic knowledge is largely implicit, being virtually contained within the experience of a single individual. In the same climate of thought we may consider the faith of any of the world's great religious systems. On the whole, people who share a psychic awareness have a common sympathy; they are more aware of their own foibles and those of their friends, and they cease to be ridiculously censorious about the shortcomings of other people and far less judgemental. It is peculiarly right that a person with genuine psychic gifts should be called a 'sensitive' rather than a medium, because sensitivity if properly cultivated can be of distinct value as part of the discernment

133

of spirits, whereas mediumship thrusts itself in front of the assembled throng as it claims its ability to make contact with the dead (a dubious claim to say the least as well as being a thoroughly dangerous one).

For the psychic gift to be of real use to humanity, both it and humanity need to be educated. It must be delivered from the glamour of revelling in phenomena that seduce the soul from its work with God on behalf of a largely deluded humanity, so that it looks for any stimulus that takes its attention off the problems confronting it in the present moment and concerns itself only in its own comfort. Thus do many people who are psychically gifted behave, abusing their gift for purely personal gain, whether for money, power, social notoriety or sensual pleasure. Humanity has likewise to be educated to the serious issues around psychism: that it is neither mental delusion nor systematized fraud; neither primitive superstition nor the antics of a sophisticated generation; neither inevitably evil like black magic nor the casting out of malign spells, nor attempting to determine or influence the future by occult techniques. Psychism is much more commonplace than all this compendium of nonsense; it is simply a way that God has made available for us to come to him directly when we lose ourselves in the concern we ought to have for our fellow creatures. When we lose concern for self to the exclusion of all other beings, we come close to the Creator of all beings. When we cease to be anything we start to become everything, since to quote once more from Ephesians 4.25, we all belong to one another, as parts of one body.

CAVEAT

It seems to me that no one devoid of a special psychic gift or sensitivity should get involved in the subject. If they are stalwart in their faith they will soon move to more fruitful fields. But if their character is weak and more suggestible – by which I mean open to suggestion or imagination – they may be dangerously vulnerable to psychic influxes from other people or even the general environment. Let me say at once that I do not feel in any way hostile either to genuinely psychic people or the subject of psychism in general. As an acutely psychic subject myself, much involved in the ministry of deliverance as well as counselling on a broader base, I would be denying something which I believe God has given me, if I were to avert my gaze from the subject. There are, however, many other gifts apart from psychic ones. Artistic ones come immediately to mind, as do also intellectual and social ones. In all of these there is some psychic component, but it is not the major one. Social skills certainly need a degree of intuition, which is not so far distant from a psychic sensitivity. Unconscious communication, which is how Jung defined intuition, clearly has much in common with psychic sensitivity, especially telepathy. There needs to be a firmer connection between depth psychology and parapsychology if either is to advance as much as it might.

As in all somewhat arcane (mysterious or hidden) matters, there is a considerable prejudice between those who are interested (nearly always a mark of some past experience) and those who are compulsively sceptical. In the latter group one may find many medical practitioners, psychologists, and even parapsychologists, who are out to prove that the subject is a completely fallacious one. To my mind the importance of psychic sensitivity at the present time is to keep people's minds open to greater possibilities than pure materialistic science. What goes by the name of religion, on the other hand, is often pure superstition based on dogmatic teaching of a past era. Here once more psychic sensitivity can help the person to move beyond the assumptions and prejudices of their group, and enter fresh fields of enquiry. The person who is genuinely sensitive psychically is less likely to fall victim either to religious fanaticism or to some occult group manipulated by a demonic figure, whether masquerading as a human or one showing its true colours in the non-material realm of a spiritual entity. These show themselves by the powerful effect they exert on a person's thinking and emotional responses; in other words they interfere with the cognitive function in a dramatic and radical manner.